White Out

Brill Guides to Scholarship in Education

Series Editors

William M. Reynolds (*Georgia Southern University, USA*)
Brad Porfilio (*Seattle University, USA*)

Editorial Board

Donna Alvermann (*University of Georgia, USA*)
Antonia Darder (*Loyola Marymount University, USA*)
Petar Jandrić (*Tehničko veleučilište u Zagrebu, Croatia*)
Lagarrett J. King (*University of Missouri, USA*)
Sherell McArthur (*University of Georgia, USA*)
William F. Pinar (*University of British Columbia, Canada*)
Pauline Sameshima (*Lakehead University, Canada*)
Christine Sleeter (*California State University Monterey Bay, USA*)

VOLUME 3

The titles published in this series are listed at *brill.com/bgse*

White Out

A Guidebook for Teaching and Engaging with Critical Whiteness Studies

By

Jennifer Beech

BRILL
SENSE

LEIDEN | BOSTON

All chapters in this book have undergone peer review.

Library of Congress Cataloging-in-Publication Data

Names: Beech, Jennifer, author.
Title: White out : a guidebook for teaching and engaging with critical whiteness studies / by Jennifer Beech.
Description: Leiden ; Boston : Brill Sense, 2020. | Series: Brill guides to scholarship in education, 2590-1958 ; volume 3 | Includes bibliographical references.
Identifiers: LCCN 2020014364 (print) | LCCN 2020014365 (ebook) | ISBN 9789004430280 (paperback) | ISBN 9789004376328 (hardback) | ISBN 9789004430297 (ebook)
Subjects: LCSH: Whites--Race identity--United States. | Whites--Race identity--Study and teaching--United States. | Racism--United States. | Racism--Study and teaching--United States.
Classification: LCC E184.A1 B336 2020 (print) | LCC E184.A1 (ebook) | DDC 305.800973--dc23
LC record available at https://lccn.loc.gov/2020014364
LC ebook record available at https://lccn.loc.gov/2020014365

Typeface for the Latin, Greek, and Cyrillic scripts: "Brill". See and download: brill.com/brill-typeface.

ISSN 2590-1958
ISBN 978-90-04-43028-0 (paperback)
ISBN 978-90-04-37632-8 (hardback)
ISBN 978-90-04-43029-7 (e-book)

Copyright 2020 by Koninklijke Brill NV, Leiden, The Netherlands.
Koninklijke Brill NV incorporates the imprints Brill, Brill Hes & De Graaf, Brill Nijhoff, Brill Rodopi, Brill Sense, Hotei Publishing, mentis Verlag, Verlag Ferdinand Schöningh and Wilhelm Fink Verlag.
All rights reserved. No part of this publication may be reproduced, translated, stored in a retrieval system, or transmitted in any form or by any means, electronic, mechanical, photocopying, recording or otherwise, without prior written permission from the publisher.
Authorization to photocopy items for internal or personal use is granted by Koninklijke Brill NV provided that the appropriate fees are paid directly to The Copyright Clearance Center, 222 Rosewood Drive, Suite 910, Danvers, MA 01923, USA. Fees are subject to change.

This book is printed on acid-free paper and produced in a sustainable manner.

Contents

Preface VII
List of Illustrations VIII

PART 1
Overview of Theory and Resources

1 **Introduction to Critical Whiteness Studies** 3
   1 What Is the Purpose and Function of CWS? 3
   2 Is CWS an Attack on White People? 3
   3 What Are the Scholarly Origins of CWS? 4
   4 Aren't We Post-Racial? Why Is CWS Still Needed? 5
   5 Where Does the Term "White" Come From? 7
   6 But I Am Not Racist, so Why Do I Need CWS 7
   7 What If I Don't Feel Privileged? Or—Conversely—How Do I Respond to Those Who Deny Privilege? 7
   8 Are Universities Actually Offering Courses Dedicated to CWS? 8
   9 Has CWS Made Its Way beyond the Academy? 9
   10 What's Next for CWS? 9

2 **Bills, Cases, Conventions, Laws, and Orders** 11

3 **Web Resources** 15

PART 2
Pedagogical Resources

4 **Activities for Structuring a Dialogic Classroom or Workshop** 21
   1 The Importance of Establishing Boundaries and Considerations for Engagement 21
   2 The Usefulness of Varying Discussion Facilitators and Recorders 21
   3 Using Reading Responses to Prepare for and Facilitate Discussions 22
   4 Introducing the Concepts of White Privilege and Implicit Bias 22
   5 Using Research Comedy to Examine Racist Policies and Practices 23

5 **Sample Syllabus** 24
   1 Rhetorics of Whiteness 24

6 Sample Assignments with Sample Student Texts   33
   1   Considerations for Writing Short Responses   33
   2   Sample Response   34
   3   Facilitation Guidelines   37
   4   Book Review Assignment   38
   5   Sample Book Review   39
   6   Sample Review of Book Read in Electronic Format   43
   7   Memoir or Critical Dialogue   46
   8   Sample Memoir   48
   9   Sample Memoir   53
   10 Sample Critical Dialogue   59
   11 Second Sample Critical Dialogue   64
   12 Cultural Studies Rhetorical Analysis Assignment   74
   13 Sample Cultural Studies Rhetorical Analysis   78

Glossary   91
Bibliography   100

Preface

Since the mid-2000's, I have been teaching a course in Critical Whiteness Studies (CWS) entitled Rhetorics of Whiteness, and though I have adopted different course texts and readers over the years, certain social, political, and legal concepts have remained part of the critical discourse. Often when someone is new to CWS, they may not have a working knowledge of, for instance, which court case originally established the Separate but Equal doctrine (or which one corrected it) or what writers mean when they trouble the concept of color blindness. Sometimes, writers and facilitators will pause to provide definitions or to discuss certain cases; other times, they won't. This guidebook, then, is designed to orient those new to Critical Whiteness Studies to its history and purpose, to key concepts and legal cases, and to established and newer texts. For those with previous exposure to CWS, this guidebook provides a quick reference and alerts them to newer texts and materials—especially to the growing body of resources now available on the Internet. For professors in any number of disciplines—particularly those wishing to offer a CWS course for their first time or for the first time on their campus—the Introduction and extensive Bibliography may prove useful in supporting the need for and validity of courses in Critical Whiteness Studies. Likewise, teachers and workshop facilitators may benefit from some of the lessons I have learned from years of working with different students and addressing issues of participation and classroom decorum (see Pedagogical Resources); students may appreciate understanding the rationale behind various pedagogical methods. Every time I teach Rhetorics of Whiteness, I am careful to strike a balance between content knowledge regarding Critical Whiteness Studies and attention to literacy development, so readers may notice that assignments are tied with genre conventions and offer invention heuristics.

This guidebook is not meant to offer a stand-alone curriculum or to provide a definitive glossary and bibliography, for that is impossible. As noted in the Introduction, professors in departments ranging from Political Science to Education to Women and Gender Studies to English and Rhetoric are offering courses in CWS, each taking their own focus and necessarily leaving out texts that others find essential. Sadly, each year, we witness new and horrific acts committed by white supremacists or encounter new hate groups and hate speech. Despite hopeful—though problematic—proclamations about the end of racism with the election of our first African-American President, we are witnessing a backlash and renewed racism at this point in American and global history. Put simply, CWS has as much exigency and kairos now as ever.

Illustrations

Figures

6.1 The Power of Four (https://m.media-amazon.com/images/M/ MV5BNjA3MDFlZTQtYzdlZC00MzQxLWE4N2QtZjFiNzRlNmRkZDJiX kEyXkFqcGdeQXVyNjMxNzQ2NTQ@._V1_.jpg).   79
6.2 Professor Utonium (https://vignette.wikia.nocookie.net/powerpuff/images/f/f6/ Utonium.gif/revision/latest/scale-to-width-down/340?cb=20130517084054).   81
6.3 Townsville (https://i.pinimg.com/originals/7f/81/d3/ 7f81d38e7c6601fd4249b972e2f6cc82.jpg).   82
6.4 Mojo Jojo (https://vignette.wikia.nocookie.net/powerpuff/images/c/c9/Mojo_ jojo_aparincia2.png/revision/latest?cb=20160612021838).   84

Table

5.1 Weekly agenda.   28

PART 1

Overview of Theory and Resources

∴

CHAPTER 1

Introduction to Critical Whiteness Studies

1 What Is the Purpose and Function of CWS?

Critical Whiteness Studies is an interdisciplinary project—with scholars from legal studies, literature and rhetorical studies, film and visual studies, class and feminist studies, etc.—that contributes to critical race theory. As Gregory Jay explains in his Whiteness Blog (2007) scholars in the field attempt

> to trace the economic and political history behind the invention of 'whiteness,' to challenge the privileges given to so-called 'whites,' and to analyze the cultural practices (in art, music, literature, and popular media) that create and perpetuate the fiction of 'whiteness.'

In their introduction to the *Rhetoric Review* Symposium on "Whiteness Studies" Kennedy, Middleton, and Ratcliffe (2005) note the cultural situatedness of the field: "Critical race studies takes its name from its function, which is to critique race and whiteness as they play out, paradoxically through visibility and invisibility, in US culture" (361). Scholars tend to posit whiteness as an ideological, political, legal, and social fiction that places so-called whites in a position of hegemony over other non-dominant groups. The project, then, functions to unmask and interrogate these fictions. As part of critical multi-cultural and race theory, the project is anti-oppressive.

2 Is CWS an Attack on White People?

No. The project attempts to help people of all races think critically about how race functions systemically and often subconsciously to privilege people with certain perceived skin traits. As Gregory Jay (2007) puts it,

> Thus it includes examining how white skin preference insinuates itself into the culture of communities of color as well, where we may find everything from prejudice against darker skinned people within the community to commercial practices of white-body imitation and surgery (nose jobs, skin creams, eyelid alteration, etc.).

Drawing upon the work of Frantz Fanon in the preface to their recent collection *Rhetorics of Whiteness: Postracial Hauntings in Popular Culture, Social Media, and Education*, Kennedy, Middleton, and Ratcliffe (2017) add, "To eradicate whiteness is not to eradicate those who claim identities as whites but rather their position of dominance in the world and the prescription of their ways of being and knowing as normal, civilized, moral—in short, human" (xvi). With a more complex understanding of how race functions within any culture, we are better able to participate in anti-racist projects that work towards more ethical practices and structures.

3 What Are the Scholarly Origins of CWS?

Certainly, people of color—W.E.B. Du Bois, James Baldwin, Zora Neal Hurston, Gloria Anzaldua, among others—were writing about racism and white power long before there were terms for identifying critical race theory. As David R. Roediger (1998) reminds us in his Preface and Introduction to the collection *Black on White: Black Writers on What it Means to Be White*, "The tendency of many writers to believe that 'whiteness studies' is a recent creation in which white scholars have pioneered thus runs directly counter to my experience" (xi). Roediger adds, "When Langston Hughes published *The Ways of White Folks* some sixty years after the end of slavery, he featured a story 'Slave on the Block' near the book's outset"—a story which highlighted the necessity for slaves to critically study potential white owners (3). Hence, from slavery on, African-Americans have a long tradition of observing, studying, and writing about whiteness and whites. Early pioneers in the field of Critical Whiteness Studies were legal scholars, literary critics, and scholars working in "white trash" studies. In fact, many of the texts included in Richard Delgado and Jean Stefancic's edited collection *Critical Whiteness Studies: Looking Behind the Mirror* (1997) are reprints of articles published in law journals in the early 1990's: pieces like Cheryl L. Harris' (1997) *Harvard Law Review* article, "Whiteness as Property" and Thomas Ross' (1990) pieces on "White Innocence and Black Abstraction" and "The Rhetorical Tapestry of Race," originally published in *William and Mary Law Review*. These articles, along with important works, like Patricia Williams' (1991) *The Alchemy of Race and Rights* and Derrick Bell's (1992) *Faces at the Bottom of the Well* became widely read and cited by scholars in other fields, especially by literature and rhetoric scholars. Toni Morrison's (1992) *Playing in the Dark: Whiteness and the Literary Imagination* broke ground

INTRODUCTION TO CRITICAL WHITENESS STUDIES 5

for literary studies, unmasking whiteness as a major trope in American literature and giving us a framework for considering bodies themselves as troped. Further, scholars like those included in Matt Wray and Annalee Newitz's (1997) collection *White Trash: Race and Class in America* helped us understand how whiteness becomes especially visible when it intersects with class. In 1993 under the editorship of John Garvey and Noel Ignatiev, the journal *Race Traitor* was established to explore race in U.S. culture. Meanwhile, scholars of color in composition and rhetoric (Ellen Cushman, Keith Gilyard, Min Zhan Lu, Malea Powell, Victor Villanueva, Jr., etc.) had taken up language and race since the early 1990's, followed by pieces like Catherine Prendergast's "Race: The Absent Presence in Composition Studies" (1998) and Krista Ratcliffe's "Rhetorical Listening: A Trope for the Interpretive Invention and a Code of Cross-Cultural Conduct" (1999) (both published in *College Composition and Communication*); these eventually lead to the 2005 *Rhetoric Review* Symposium on "Whiteness Studies." Since this early work, CWS has been taken up in education journals, by cultural studies and film scholars, by non-fiction writers exploring intersections of race, class, gender, sexual orientation, etc., as well as by critical race scholars making their work widely available on the Internet (see the Bibliography and the online resources sections included in this book).

4   Aren't We Post-Racial? Why Is CWS Still Needed?

After the election of Barack Obama to the highest office in the United States, many pundits declared us to be in a post-racial era where race supposedly no longer mattered. However, as history has shown us repeatedly, when non-dominant groups make even the slightest gains towards equality, a backlash follows. Annette Harris Powell (2017) reminds us, "Accordingly, many of the civil rights gains of the 1960's have been dismantled through colorblind policies. The appeal of colorblind neutrality and postracialism rests in the fact that race can be submerged so that any substantive or critical discussion of race is avoided" (19). CWS repeatedly uncovers how claims of colorblindness and declarations of being post-racial work to mask implicit and systemic racism. Certainly, when recent world leaders have run explicitly racist campaigns maligning people of color as rapists, thugs, and threats, and as people of color are repeatedly singled out, brutalized, and killed by law enforcement, race and whiteness are terms that have become unavoidable in the public discourse. Anti-racist activists must now grapple with a new wave of anti-immigration policies and overt, as well as thinly coded, racist rhetoric in the wake of Brexit and the policies of the Trump administration. With a recent rise in hate crimes and white nationalism, Critical Whiteness Studies is needed now as much as it ever was. According to the FBI's reporting, as required by the Hate Crimes Statistics Act, 2017 marked the third consecutive year for a noted increase in hate crimes. During 2017, hate crimes in general increased 17%, while anti-black hate crimes saw a 16% increase from 2016. According to a March 20, 2019 post from FactCheck.Org, the following are additional indicators that white nationalism and white supremacy are on the rise in the U.S.:

– The Southern Poverty Law Center reports a dramatic increase in the number of white nationalist groups in the U.S., from 100 chapters in 2017 to 148 in 2018.
– The Anti-Defamation League reports a 182% increase in incidents of the distribution of white supremacist propaganda, and an increase in the number of rallies and demonstrations by white supremacy groups, from 76 in 2017 to 91 in 2018.
– A study by the Center for Strategic and International Studies found the number of terrorist attacks by far-right perpetrators quadrupled in the U.S. between 2016 and 2017, and that far-right attacks in Europe rose 43% over the same period. Among those incidents, CSIS states, the rise of attacks by white supremacists and anti-government extremists is "of particular concern" ("The Facts on White Nationalism," featured post by Robert Farley).

Four recent high-profile travesties make starkly clear the dangers inherent in the rise in white nationalism:

1. The first, which took place in June 2015, involved the murder of nine African Americans and injury of one other participant of a prayer group at Emanuel African Methodist Episcopal Church in Charleston, South Carolina by a professed white supremacist who explicitly said the act was designed to ignite a race war.
2. In August 2017, a white nationalist plowed his car into a crowd of protestors at the Unite the Right march in Charlottesville, Virginia, killing one woman and injuring 19 more.
3. The third was the 2018 shooting at the Tree of Life Synagogue in Pittsburg, in which a white nationalist gunned down 11 Jewish people.
4. The shooting of 51 people at a mosque in Christchurch, New Zealand, in March 2019 by a professed white supremacist further evidences the rise of white nationalism on a global scale.

Critical Whiteness Studies is necessary for helping us historicize the role of whiteness in individual and systemic acts of oppression and for providing us with the tools for dismantling and fighting oppressive thinking, acts, and systems. We need this work to help us think and act critically.

5 Where Does the Term "White" Come From?

Respected scholars Theodore W. Allen (*The Invention of the White Race*, 1994), Gregory Jay ("Who Invented White People," 2007), and Tim Wise (*On White Privilege: Racism, White Denial, and Costs of Inequality*, 2008) note that prior to the seventeenth century, colonial Americans did not use the term "white race." It only began to appear as a social and legal term in the late 1660's/early 1670's as wealthy whites employed a divide and conquer strategy to break up alliances between poor white and black indentured servants. Elites in Virginia began to offer poor whites freedom from indentured servitude, as well as 50 acres of land, if they would act as "white" slave patrols to reign in any black rebellions.

6 But I Am Not Racist, so Why Do I Need CWS?

Simply declaring yourself not racist or not wanting to be racist is not enough. Critical race theorists find the binary of racist-not racist somewhat unproductive and encourage us to think of people existing somewhere along a continuum: with extreme racism on one end and those harboring more implicit racism on the other end. We may all be racist but to different degrees. This is the impetus behind such endeavors as Harvard's Project Implicit, which provides several IATs (Implicit Association Tests). Because of cultural messaging that we may have absorbed throughout our lives, we all likely harbor at least some implicit stereotypes, bigotry, and forms of oppressive thinking—be they based upon gender, sexual orientation, religion, race, national origin, ethnicity, disability, etc. CWS provides us with the tools for thinking in critical ways about race, for unpacking and exposing our implicit associations, and for becoming actively anti-racist.

7 What If I Don't Feel Privileged? Or—Conversely—How Do I Respond to Those Who Deny Privilege?

It's important to understand the difference between individual feelings and experiences and larger structures of power and privilege. As Michael Zweig (2012) writes in *The Working-Class Majority: America's Best Kept Secret*, most Americans are in the working class—even as the myth of the U.S. as a classless society persists. Many poor and working-class white people certainly do not feel privileged. Likewise, plenty of people from non-dominant groups experience oppression—either in individual acts or in structural systems. Peggy McIntosh's (1989) "White Privilege: Unpacking the Invisible Knapsack" is a good primer for understanding how white privilege operates systemically—sometimes in larger structures (as in gerrymandering), others times in micro-aggressions (someone clutching their purse when a person of color walks by the car). Being a member of a privileged group does not equate with feeling empowered on a daily basis. Likewise, we all occupy multiple subjectivities simultaneously (see "Intersectionality" in the Glossary). Women from all backgrounds still face a glass ceiling with respect to wages and advancement. People in the LGBTQIA community face a myriad of individual and structural assaults. To understand how privilege operates, we have to be open to critical inquiry and to potential discomfort as we examine harsh realities. Here's where the concept of rhetorical listening is key (see "Rhetorical listening" in the Glossary). In *Rhetorical Listening: Identification, Gender, and Whiteness*, Krista Ratcliffe (2005) outlines a theory that positions listening itself as a rhetorical act. In a recent a blog post from June 13, 2019, entitled "Checking Privilege," anti-racist activist Tim Wise notes that it can be unproductive to view others as attempting to derail conversations about white privilege when they speak of incidents of oppression they have faced. Wise notes the importance of letting "people talk about the complexity of their identities and [taking] an intersectional approach with the folks we hope to reach." Listening shows empathy and goodwill and, in turn, invites it. He goes on, "When someone mentions how they've been marginalized by their class status, for instance, it opens up the discussion about how those who haven't experienced economic hardship have the privilege of not understanding what that's like. Then, the person who understandably detests the obliviousness of the affluent can be steered back to their own obliviousness about whiteness, helping to clarify the point you were hoping to make in the first place." Likewise, in their discussion of allyship, the Anti-Oppressive Network (2019) identifies listening as a key concept for white people wishing to engage in the life-long process of allyship: "we must listen more and speak less: we hold back on our ideas, opinions, and ideologies, and resist the urge to 'save' the people we seek to work with...." A famous quote often attributed to the Dalai Lama is worth minding: "When you talk, you are only repeating what you already know. But if you listen, you may learn something new."

8   Are Universities Actually Offering Courses Dedicated to CWS?

Yes. While many colleges and universities incorporate diversity readers in first-year courses, most full-blown CWS courses are offered as upper-level

undergraduate and/or graduate courses in departments ranging from Political Science to Education to Religion to Gender and Ethnic Studies to English. What follows is but a sampling of course titles offered across the United States:
- *Critical Whiteness Studies*, Department of American Studies and Ethnicity, University of Southern California; also offered by, Communication and Rhetorical Studies, Syracuse.
- *Deconstructing Whiteness*, Democratic Education, University of California.
- *Power and Privilege*, Graduate Certificate Program in Diversity, Social Justice, and Inclusion, University of Colorado Springs.
- *Problematizing Whiteness*, Political Science, University of Colorado Denver.
- *The Problem of Whiteness*, African Cultural Studies, University of Wisconsin-Madison.
- *Rhetorics of Whiteness*, English Department, University of Tennessee, Chattanooga.

It is worth noting that these courses sometimes attract the attention and criticism of conservative politicians and media—which makes a guidebook like this one a useful resource for pointing to the rich academic tradition of, as well as the exigency for, Critical Whiteness Studies.

9 Has CWS Made Its Way beyond the Academy?

Yes, in a variety of important ways. Feminist educator and activist Peggy McIntosh's (1989) "White Privilege: Unpacking the Invisible Knapsack" is widely available on the Internet and is often used in community, law enforcement, and other workshops, as well as in high school and college classrooms. Several whiteness scholar-activists—most notably Tim Wise and Michael Eric Dyson—have become public intellectuals, regularly appearing as guest commentators/speakers on network news, PBS, and NPR, as well as writing books that bridge academic and popular audiences (see Bibliography and Web Resources). As evidenced by the Web Resources section of this guidebook, the number of anti-racist coalitions and non-profits has been growing; these provide local, as well as web, resources. With respect to organized religion, Unitarian Universalist Allies for Racial Equity is exemplary for their website and anti-racist curriculum, activities, and tools for enacting allyship (see Web Resources).

10 What's Next for CWS?

Now well into the twenty-first century, we can observe several developments that merit either renewed or completely new attention from the perspective of

CWS. As more evidence of foreign election interference emerges, it becomes clear that social media has become a major avenue for disseminating messages of white supremacy and other racist tropes. Much work is left to be done in digital and media studies—not simply to uncover the ways that propaganda is distributed, but also for thinking about how social media and streaming services (think Netflix's limited series *When They See Us*) might be better employed for the purposes of anti-racist work. So, while CWS scholars should continue their mission of unmasking how the fiction of whiteness works to oppress, we need also to examine ways to mobilize for collective action (think leaderless protest movements like Black Lives Matter, Me Too, and Hong Kong citizens). In their "Epilogue" to *Rhetorics of Whiteness*, Kennedy, Middleton, and Ratcliffe (2017) call for a renewed attention to *intersectionality*: "For example we might study the white Latino/as in the United States (one of whom was running for the 2016 GOP nomination), white LGBTQIA's, and issues of colorism that are growing generally in the United States as well as their representation in television and film media" (311). More attention to race as it intersects with class, disability, sexuality, gender, and other subjectivities is needed—particularly in light of neoliberal policies that mask white supremacy, as well as heteronormative and other structures of domination that work under the guise of common sense public policy. More attention is needed with respect to the rise in populism and anti-immigration rhetoric. As journalists and ordinary citizens grapple over whether or not it is appropriate to call someone or a particular policy "racist," we need a renewed discussion about what racism is, how it works, and the harm that it does.

CHAPTER 2

Bills, Cases, Conventions, Laws, and Orders

Arizona House Bill 2281 (2010)
Signed into law on May 11, 2010 by Arizona Governor Jan Brewer, this law prohibited courses that promoted the overthrow of the U.S. government, instilled racial resentment, or were designed for students of a particular ethnic group. Recognized widely as a purpose effort to shut down Mexican American Studies, a federal judge in 2017 ruled this law unconstitutional.

Brown v. Board of Education of Topeka, 374 U.S. 483 (1954) (Separate is not equal)
Landmark case in which the Supreme Court unanimously ruled that separate schools for black and white children was unconstitutional. The case was filed by Oliver Brown after his daughter was denied entry to an all-white elementary school in Topeka. The lawsuit claimed that school segregation violated the equal protection clause of the 14th Amendment.

Chinese Exclusion Act & Geary Act (1882; 1892)
Passed in spring of 1882 and signed by President Chester A. Arthur, this act prohibited Chinese labor immigration for ten years, placed new restrictions on Chinese people already residing in the U.S., and prohibited state and federal courts from granting citizenship to Chinese residents. Under this act, which was extended in 1892 under the Geary Act, Chinese residents were also required to register or face deportation, and if they left the country, they were not guaranteed reentry. It was not until 1943 that Congress repealed all exclusion acts.

Deferred Action for Childhood Arrivals (DACA) (Executive Branch Memorandum)
On June 15, 2012, President Barack Obama issued this memorandum, which allows children who came to the U.S. before age 16 to apply for a two-year renewable extension that allows them to remain in the country.

Executive Order 10025 (1961)
An order issued by President John F. Kennedy mandating federal contractors and subcontractors to take affirmative action to avoid racial bias.

Executive Order 11246 (1965)
An order issued by President Lyndon Johnson upholding affirmative action as framed under the Civil Rights Act, which prohibits government contractors and subcontractors from discriminating on the basis of race, color, religion, or national origin.

Fisher v. Texas, 579 U.S.__ (2016)
Case brought by Abigail Fisher and Rachel Michalewicz against University of Texas, alleging that the school's admissions policy discriminated against them because of its inclusion of race in its Academic Index and Personal Achievement Index, especially for giving further consideration to students who were not automatically admitted because they fell below the top 10% of their high school class. The court found that because race was only one amongst a variety of factors in those indexes, the university's policy did not violate the plaintiff's equal protections.

Gratz v. Bollinger, 539 U.S. 244 (2003)
Class action law suit filed by Jennifer Gratz and Patrick Hamacher claiming that the Undergraduate Admission Office of the University of Michigan's system of granting 20 automatic points to African-American and Native-American students was discriminatory against white students and violated their equal protections. The Supreme Court ruled 6–3 that the point system was unconstitutional because it "ensures that the diversity contributions of applicants cannot be individually accessed."

Grutter v. Bollinger, 539 U.S. 306 (2003)
Landmark case in which the Supreme Court upheld by a 5–4 decision the Affirmative Action admissions policies of the University of Michigan Law School. Barbara Grutter, a white student with a 3.8 GPA and 161 LSAT score, brought the suit when denied admission. Unlike the undergraduate admissions policy, which granted 20 automatic points to underrepresented minorities, the law school used race as only one of a number of factors, allowing for—the court argued—the close scrutiny called for under equal protections.

Hate Crimes Statistics Act, 28 U.S.C. 534 (1990), modified in 2009 by the Matthew Shepard and James Byrd, Jr. Hate Crimes Prevention Act
Signed into law by President George H. W. Bush, this law requires the Attorney General of the U.S. to collect data on crimes committed because of a victim's race, religion, disability, sexual orientation, or ethnicity. The second law,

expanded HCSA, as well as federal hate crimes laws, to include a victim's actual or perceived gender, sexual orientation, gender identity, or disability.

International Convention on the Elimination of All Forms of Racial Discrimination

This United Nations Convention was adopted in 1965 and began to be enforced in 1969. It defines racial discrimination as "any distinction, exclusion, restriction or preference based on race, colour, descent, or national or ethnic origin which has the purpose or effect of nullifying or impairing the recognition, enjoyment or exercise, on an equal footing, of human rights and fundamental freedoms in the political, economic, social, cultural or any other field in public life."

Loving v. Virginia, 388 U.S. 1 (1967)

Landmark case in which the Supreme Court ruled unanimously that laws prohibiting interracial marriage violated the Due Process Clause and Equal Protection Clause of the 14th Amendment. The case was brought by Mildred Loving, a woman of color, and Richard Loving, a white man, who were arrested and found guilty of violating Virginia's Racial Integrity Act of 1924.

Naturalization Act of 1790

The first act defining citizenship rules for the U.S.; it allowed only white persons who had lived in the country for at least two years and was designed to exclude Native Americans, Asians, current or former slaves, and most women (women could accompany a husband or adult son if his application were approved).

Naturalization Act of 1870; Naturalization Act of 1906

This act placed more control at the federal level than did the one of 1790 and extended naturalization to persons of African descent. It codified the naturalization process, along with penalties for those who violated it. The 1906 act, signed into law by Theodore Roosevelt, added the requirement that immigrants learn English. It was repealed and replaced by the Nationality Act of 1940. A number of acts related to immigration followed.

Philadelphia Order (1969)

An order issued by President Richard Nixon, using the city of Philadelphia as a test case, which gave the city's unions and construction industry goals and timetables, but not quotas, for demonstrating affirmative action in order to increase employment of minorities.

Plessy v. Ferguson, 163 U.S. 537 (1896) (Singular segregation)
A landmark case that is widely regarded as one of the worst decisions of the Supreme Court. The court ruled 7–1 that racial segregations laws for public facilities were constitutional as long as the facilities were supposedly equal in quality. The case was brought by Homer Plessy, a person of mixed race, after he was arrested for sitting in the all-whites section of a rail car in New Orleans; in 1890, Louisiana had passed the Separate Car Act, which Plessy was found in violation of.

Reconstruction Amendments/Civil War Amendments (13th, 14th, and 15th)
- 13th, ratified on December 1865, this amendment abolished slavery.
- 14th, ratified on July 9, 1868, this amendment granted citizenship to all persons born or naturalized in the U.S., including former slaves, and provided all citizens with equal protection under the law.
- 15th, ratified on February 3, 1870, this amendment prohibited states from disenfranchising voters on account of race, color, or previous conditions of servitude.

Regents of the University of California v. Bakke, 438 U.S. 265 (1978)
Landmark case in which the Supreme Court ruled 5–1 to uphold affirmative action, which allows race to be an admission factor, but ruling that admissions quotas were not permissible because they violated the Equal Protection Clause of the 14th Amendment. The case was brought by Allan Bakke, a white man in his 30's, after he was refused admittance by the University of California, Davis; Davis had a policy of reserving 16 out of 100 seats for minority students.

United Nations International Day for the Elimination of Racial Discrimination (March 21)
Now observed annually, in 1966 the UN declared this day as a remembrance of the day in 1960 when 69 peaceful protestors (of apartheid laws) were gunned down by police in Sharpeville, South Africa. The day reminds UN members to redouble their efforts to fight racial discrimination.

CHAPTER 3

Web Resources

Alliance of White Anti-Racists Everywhere—Los Angeles (AWARE-LA)
https://www.awarela.org
An all-volunteer alliance of white anti-racist people who organize with people of color. Their homepage has links to "Why Do We Organize White Folks?," "Get Involved," "Upcoming Events," and "Who We Do This Work With."

Anti-Oppression Network, The
https://theantioppressionnetwork.com/allyship/
Useful resource for defining allyship (for those in positions of privilege who seek solidarity with non-dominant groups), especially the roles and responsibilities of allies.

"Bibliography: Whiteness Studies." *National Writing Project*
https://www.nwp.org/cs/public/print/resource/2592
Includes academic and classroom resources.

Catalyst Project
https://collectiveliberation.org
An anti-racist project "committed to building the leadership of white people to be part of anti-racist social movements working for fundamental change." Based out of the San Francisco Bay Area, their site details their local work, but also provides an excellent Resources page, which gives "Principles for Racial Justice Activists in the Face of State Repression," curricular materials, links to educational events, links to other organizations that provide training for activists, as well as a host of other useful resources.

Center for the Study of White American Culture, Inc.
http://www.euroamerican.org/default.asp
A New Jersey-based nonprofit that provides anti-racist resources ranging from strategy papers to definitions and histories to a bookstore and blog.

Community Change, Inc. (CCI)
http://www.communitychangeinc.org
Based in Boston and founded in 1968, this organization aims "to meet the challenge of 'the White Problem.'" Their site provides descriptions of public events

they sponsor, their consulting services, and an excellent Resource Center with an email list and newsletter.

> *Examining Whiteness: An Anti-Racism Curriculum,* Unitarian Universalist Association
> https://www.uua.org/racial-justice/curricula/whiteness

A collection of material compiled by Reverend Doctor William Gardiner, designed "particularly for white people interested in transforming their whiteness through understanding the complex history of white supremacy of over four hundred years in the United States, and the impact it has on us as individuals and the society as a whole." Provides reading materials.

> Jay, Greg. *Whiteness Studies and White Privilege*
> http://studywhiteness.blogspot.com

Provides an introduction to whiteness studies with several articles by Jay, as well as articles by other critical race scholars; pedagogical resources for teaching about whiteness; bibliographic links; links to university programs that offer degrees in whiteness studies; blog posts by Jay; as well as links to his academic page.

> *Project Implicit.* Harvard University, 2011
> https://implicit.harvard.edu/implicit/

Provides implicit association tests (IATs) about race, gender, sexual orientation, and other topics.

> *Southern Poverty Law Center*
> https://www.splcenter.org

Founded in 1971 by Alabama civil rights lawyer Morris Dees, this non-profit organization works to ensure the civil rights of all, but especially of poor and underrepresented groups. The group provides pro bono legal services, conducts and publishes studies (recently, one on Confederate monuments), and serves as a general watchdog against oppressive laws and civil rights violations. Particularly pertinent to whiteness studies is their "Hatewatch" blog and their "Extremist Files," which monitor and document the activities of hate groups.

> SPAN: *Safehouse Progressive Alliance for Nonviolence*
> https://www.safehousealliance.org

While primarily designed to provide education, counseling, legal services, and support for victims of domestic violence, this nonprofit also works for inclusivity and social justice in general.

Race Forward
https://www.raceforward.org
A combination of two previously separate organizations—The Center for Racial Justice Innovation and Center for Social Inclusion—has a "mission to build awareness, solutions, and leadership for racial justice by generating transformative ideas, information, and experiences." Their site provides research and tool kits, such as "Adding Racial Equity to the Menu: An Equity Toolkit for Restaurant Employers" to videos explaining what systemic racism is. They also sponsor a daily news site on race, called "Colorlines."

Racial Equality Tools
https://www.racialequitytools.org/home
A site "designed to support individuals and groups working to achieve racial equity" with resources designed to move anti-racist activists from knowledge to action. They provide action plans, as well as curricula.

Teaching Tolerance
https://www.tolerance.org
An excellent resource for K-12 school teachers, providing classroom resources, professional development opportunities, research reports, links to grants, etc.

Tim Wise.org
http://www.timwise.org
The site of prominent antiracist essayist, author, public intellectual, and educator. Provides: a bibliography of his books and DVDs; an essay archive; a video and audio link page, including appearances on major news networks; and links to upcoming events featuring Wise as a speaker or commentator.

"Understanding Whiteness," CARED: *Calgary Anti-Racism Education*
http://www.ucalgary.ca/cared/whiteness
Provides a useful discussion, along with bibliographic links, of the difference between "white" (a category of "race" with no biological/scientific foundation) and "whiteness" as a powerful social construct.

White Awake
https://whiteawake.org
An online platform for people socialized as white designed to combat white supremacy. Provides: analyses of race as a social construction; manuals for designing workshops and study groups, and for personal and community practices; bibliographic links to articles on such topics as racism and white

supremacy, the invention of whiteness, whiteness and class, cultural appropriation, and other important areas of whiteness study; a quarterly blog; and a page that offers consulting services.

> *"Whiteness Studies," WISE: Working to Improve Schools and Education. Ithaca College*
> https://www.ithaca.edu/wise/whiteness/

Provides numerous links for understanding whiteness studies and white privilege, including a link to Peggy McIntosh's classic 1989 article "White Privilege: Unpacking the Invisible Knapsack"; links to understanding and practicing allyship; pedagogical links; and a brief bibliography of books and articles.

> *Whites for Racial Equality*
> http://whitesforracialequity.org

An affiliate of SURJ (Showing Up for Racial Justice), is based out of Monterey County, CA, and works to move "white folks into accountable action as part of a multi-racial movement through community organizing, mobilizing and education" ("Welcome"). Their site provides links to events, a glossary of terms related to critical race studies, links to readings and activities for unpacking white privilege, and a host of other resources for educators and anti-racist activists. Under "Essential Reading/Viewing" are extremely useful pedagogical tools; in particular, "Interrupting Microaggressions" and "10 Must-Follow Racial Justice Movers and Shakers on Twitter."

> *White Noise Collective*
> https://www.conspireforchange.org

The site for a collective that is primarily based in the SF Bay Area, but with chapters in Rhode Island and New York; they emphasize seeing race, class, and gender as interlocking systems of oppression. The website provides: monthly dialogues; an overview of workshops they offer; extensive bibliographic links for understanding white privilege and systemic racism, cultural appropriation, and other important resources for understanding intersectional approaches to anti-racism activism; biographic entries on anti-racist role models; and a calendar of events sponsored by the collective.

PART 2

Pedagogical Resources

CHAPTER 4

Activities for Structuring a Dialogic Classroom or Workshop

1   The Importance of Establishing Boundaries and Considerations for Engagement

As many critical educators have noted, when course participants read about and discuss uncomfortable subjects, they benefit from a dialogic classroom where rules for engagement are mutually agreed upon and observed by participants. After introductory matters (discussing the syllabus or workshop agenda, goals, policies, etc.), participants might break into small groups to discuss considerations for productive discussions. These groups then report to the whole group, and as each new consideration is introduced—to raise hands or not, to avoid name calling, to demonstrate active listening, to avoid monopolizing the conversation, etc.—the whole group can voice concerns/objections/amendments and can vote on each proposed procedure or consideration. Professors or workshop leaders can add in considerations of their own: for example, reminding participants not to make any individuals of color "the" spokesperson for their race. These considerations can be posted in a course platform or on a poster/whiteboard and can be amended as needed as the semester/workshop progresses. Special attention might be given to notions of rhetorical listening, the need for moments of silence and reflection, and for when the professor or workshop facilitator might intervene to redirect or pause a discussion.

2   The Usefulness of Varying Discussion Facilitators and Recorders

For a dialogic classroom, the teacher or workshop coordinator can act as one facilitator and provide expertise when appropriate, but all participants can benefit by engaging in a variety of active ways. Participants might sign up to act as co-facilitators at different points in the semester. Doing so helps bring new styles of discussion and avoids making the professor or workshop organizer the central figure. Since participants often bring different classroom styles, some might volunteer to act as classroom recorders, instead of facilitators—being responsible for taking notes about what happened during a particular session, what questions or topics were left unaddressed, where an activity/discussion left off, etc. Recorder notes can be posted to the course platform and can assist those not present with catching up on what happened, as well as help all participants consider their goals for the next or future sessions. (See Facilitation Guidelines)

3   Using Reading Responses to Prepare for and Facilitate Discussions

Occasionally, the professor or organizer might assign participants to write a response to a reading or set of readings prior to coming to a session. Doing so, participants have the opportunity to structure their thoughts before simply jumping into a discussion. These responses can be read aloud by participants in small groups, followed by discussion amongst those in the group. The facilitator might set a time parameter and ask for a group representative to write on a white board 2–3 important points or questions they find worth engaging as a whole group. This can be a good way for more introverted participants to share their ideas and to have their ideas put forth to the whole group (perhaps, by a fellow group member). This activity works well for helping participants gain comfort in participating before simply jumping into a whole group discussion. (See Response Guidelines)

4   Introducing the Concepts of White Privilege and Implicit Bias

Because people often do not feel particularly privileged, an important introductory pedagogical move is to help participants understand the many levels at which privilege and bias operate both structurally and implicitly. One strategy is to ask participants during their own time (as homework) to read Peggy McIntosh's "White Privilege: Unpacking the Invisible Knapsack," as well as to take the Harvard Race Implicit Association Test. Tell them that you will not ask for their results on the IAT, but that you will ask them to take it again at the end of the semester or workshop. During the next class, watch Tim Wise's video "Train Yourself to See It" (available via his website and on YouTube). Discuss the importance of recognizing white privilege and calling out stereotyping and racial profiling, which may be rooted in both explicit and implicit biases. Have participants work in small groups to go over McIntosh's list with an eye to what may have changed since she wrote her piece. Give groups a time parameter to report back to everyone on the following: what might be taken off and/or added to the list? For instance, new additions might include: "My family and

I can barbeque in a park without having a white woman harass us and call the police on us." "My child can sell bottled water or lemonade in our neighborhood without being harassed or having the police called on her." Unfortunately, there are all too many current examples, like BBQ Becky, Permit Patty, Cornerstone Caroline, and Golfcart Gail. As a follow up to this activity, participants might debate what such monikers do or do not achieve rhetorically.

5   Using Research Comedy to Examine Racist Policies and Practices

As Michelle Lipkin, executive director of the National Association for Media Literacy Education, argues, satire affects the way we think and plays an important role in how we get our news. Satire, by its very definition, critiques social and political norms. Hence, satire can be a useful tool for unmasking and critiquing racist structures. With this in mind, professors and workshop organizers might make use of the genre of research comedy, which is now readily available on streaming services and on the Internet. Have participants watch on their own (as homework) the following two particularly well-researched sketches: Adam Ruins Everything "The Disturbing History of the Suburbs" (on redlining) and John Oliver's "Border Wall: Last Week Tonight." When they watch the videos at home, their task is simply to process the content by watching the videos at least twice and taking notes. Then, in class, participants watch the videos again but with the instructions to take notes about feature common to the genre of research comedy. Participants might first discuss the content and then spend time discussing generic considerations. This activity could be a stand-alone one or could be scaffolded to lead to an assignment that asks participants to brainstorm for or even create their own critical research sketch.

CHAPTER 5

Sample Syllabus

1   Rhetorics of Whiteness

1.1   *Course Description*
In this dialogic, student-centered *seminar*, we will interrogate the following concerns and questions:
- Notions of whiteness as a rhetorical, cultural, social, and legal construct.
- How does whiteness as a rhetorical and legal construct operate to further institutional racism?
- How can explicit classroom examinations of whiteness move conversations from personal attitudes (and guilt) to the objective analysis of historical events, legal codes, social institutions, and cultural practices?
- How do silences about whiteness let whites off the hook with respect to race relations? What are the consequences of normalizing whiteness as a racial category?
- What happens or can happen when we make whiteness visible? What becomes possible rhetorically and socially?
- Whiteness has been a significant legal and political category, and thus a powerful reality even if it is based on fantasy. Whiteness is a way of distributing wealth and power according to arbitrary notions of biological differences. Recognizing these realities, what is our responsibility as civic-minded rhetors?
- How have other writers (of various races) contributed to our understanding of whiteness and race relations?
- How might folks from a range of backgrounds unite for the purposes of justice? What place do thoughtful rhetorics of whiteness have within the framework of participatory democracy?
- In what ways can we use our rhetorical skills to enter into and to intervene in important private and public conversations where race is or should be a factor?

1.2   *Course Goals*
Through various readings, class discussions, and texts produced, students should seek to:

- Gain a greater understanding of whiteness as it operates in the United States, as well as consider how responsible rhetors might intervene in the construction of race and race relations.
- Gain wider exposure to and appreciation of alternative rhetorics.
- Gain a greater understanding of how the subjectivities of class, race, gender, and sexual orientation intersect with each other and inform, interfere with, and/or (under)write rhetorical acts.
- Gain exposure to a wide range of authors/thinkers on the subject of whiteness.
- Gain or increase skills for analyzing and engaging with rhetorical artifacts.
- Gain/increase exposure to scholarly discussions about identity politics within the fields of Rhetoric and Composition and Critical Whiteness Studies.
- Further one's ability as a rhetor and rhetorician, employing a range of appropriate rhetorical appeals, genres, and formats as determined appropriate for intended audiences.
- Push self as writer, taking risks with topics, form(at), tone, style, and various rhetorical strategies.

1.3   Required Texts
- *Rhetorics of Whiteness: Postracial Hauntings in Popular Culture, Social Media, and Education.*
- *White Out: A Guidebook for Teaching and Engaging with Critical Whiteness Studies.*
- Roediger, David R. *Black on White: Black Writers on What it Means to be White* (excerpts).
- Various handouts, as well as readings linked through through the course platform.
- One book each selected for individual book review.

1.4   Course Requirements and Grade Distribution
1. (10%) *Responses to Readings*: Each of these must be typed and at least three paragraphs: paragraph 1) summarize the author's points to which you wish to respond; paragraph 2) analyze how the author communicates his/her message (pay attention to rhetorical strategies employed); and paragraph 3) personalize your discussion by adding in your thoughts and experiences, arguing with or against the authors, or otherwise adding your well-reasoned points to the conversation.

2. (20%) *Book Review*: You will each read and present a review of a full-length book that addresses whiteness. The professor will provide a list of acceptable texts. The purpose of the review is to encourage you to read an intellectual discussion of whiteness in relation to rhetoric, but also to educate the rest of us about what kind of work on whiteness is out there; these reviews allow us as a class wider exposure to the larger conversation than we each could read individually. Remember that a review is not merely a summary, but is a critical analysis of the author's central arguments, as well as a commentary about the efficacy of the discussion and potential audiences for the book.

3. (20%) *Memoir or Critical Dialogue*: (6–8 pp for undergrads; 8–10 for grads) For this assignment, you may either compose a memoir exploring your own encounter or experience with race (being read as white; being privileged as white; reading others as white; encountering white privilege in others; mistrusting someone due to their perceived race, etc.) *OR* create a dialogue between the writer-thinkers we will read this semester.

    For the memoir—Situate/position/narrate yourself as a person with a particular racial history experience; explore a moment or related moments of concord/dissonance/rupture in your encounters with self or others as racially constructed beings. (Note: if you choose this option, you will need to seriously think about your own racial positioning/affiliations/predicaments, etc., so be prepared to do so as honestly as possible.)

    For the dialogue—Choose a theme or topic to serve as a focus, select 3–4 voices from our readings that represent a range of perspectives on/approaches to whiteness, and compose a well-crafted conversation between them. Each "character" in your dialogue should speak for several sentences to a full paragraph each time he/she speaks and should speak at least twice. If you alter a speaker's actual words to make the conversation flow, be sure to stay true to the person's character and to note your alterations through the use of [brackets]. Each speaker should treat the other's perspective seriously, if skeptically, but with respect. You are striving for a thoughtful, balanced treatment/synthesis of the topic.

4. (20%) *Analysis of Popular Media with Respect to Whiteness*: (5.5–7 pp. for undergrads; 10–15 for grads): For this assignment, you will select a popular/media (magazine, video, t.v. program or movie, speech, catalog or billboard, etc.) representation of whiteness to analyze from a cultural studies rhetorical perspective (considering production, circulation, and reception, along with other major rhetorical appeals).

5. (20%) *Discussion Facilitations and Recordings*: In keeping with the seminar format, in which all participants (students and professor, alike)

engage the seminar topic with equal rigor and enthusiasm, each seminar participant will help lead our discussion twice in the semester. Each facilitation should last 15–20 minutes and should include at least one handout or visual. The idea is to help everyone better understand the assigned reading, to tease out nuances in the author's argument, to consider the author's rhetorical approach, and/or to synthesize the perspectives of the author with those presented in other readings. Your facilitation will be our primary time with a particular reading, so it is important that you do an excellent job of addressing the major issues the reading raises. Please keep us active and engaged by having a plan and preparing well; a 20-minutes lecture or monologue is not appropriate, nor is the lack of preparation associated with the "Okay, so what do you all think of it?" approach. Each participant will also act as the class recorder for at least one session—helping to wrap up/reflect upon a particular class discussion, as well as posting in our course Discussion Board a synopsis of major issues and insights brought up in class that day. (See guidelines for more details.)

6. (10%) *Participation + In-class or Short Homework*: As participants in an advance rhetoric and writing seminar, you should recognize the importance of active and engaged classroom citizenship to the success of any classroom. Indeed, the seminar format assumes that all participants together tackle a question or issue with intellectual rigor. This acknowledged, participants are expected (and will be graded accordingly) to assume responsibility for the collaborative knowledge-making to take place this semester by:
   - Demonstrating increasing confidence in participating in classroom and online forums.
   - Preparing thoroughly and thoughtfully for class.
   - Raising issues and questions (in class and online).
   - Facilitating and mediating small group and whole-class discussions.
   - Actively listening to and responding to other class participants, including thoughtful peer review and exhibiting a willingness to consider alternative perspectives.
   - Introducing relevant ideas, texts, and knowledge from outside the class.
   - Purposefully tackling in-class and homework style exercises.
   - Meeting deadlines.
   - Regularly and actively attending class.
   - Presenting ideas and writing in a professional, ethical, and timely manner.

TABLE 5.1 Weekly agenda

Week	Day 1	Day 2

Week 1
Introductions
	Introduction of students, professor, course descriptions, goals, policies, texts, etc. Seminar participants generate guidelines for productive class discussion.	1. Prior to class have read/watched the following:
		   – Peggy McIntosh's "White Privilege: Unpacking the Invisible Knapsack"
		   – "Introduction to CWS" (in this book)
		   – Take the Harvard IAT on Race
		2. Discuss what is out of date and/or left out of McIntosh's framework.
		3. Watch Tim Wise videos: "White Privilege" and "Train Yourself to See It"

Week 2 *Historicizing Whiteness Studies;* *Understanding Its Place in Rhet/Comp;* *Developing an Initial Vocabulary for Critical Whiteness Studies*	Prior to class have read/done the following: – *Rhetoric Review* "Symposium: Whiteness Studies" 2. Small and whole group application of key concepts.	1. Prior to class, have read assigned sections on Gregory Jay's Whiteness Studies page. 2. Begin to sign up for book reviews

(*cont.*)

SAMPLE SYLLABUS 29

TABLE 5.1 Weekly agenda (*cont.*)

Week	Day 1	Day 2
Week 3 *How whites as dominant group members (fail to) see racism; and the perspectives of people of color; whiteness as terror/violence/privilege*	1. Prior to class, have read the following: – Critical Whiteness Studies pp. xvii–47 Facilitator: – *Black on White* pp. 3–53 Facilitator: 2. Discuss differing perspectives on how people see whites depending upon their own racial affiliations.	1. Prior to class, have read – In *Rhetorics of Whiteness*: "Whiteness as Racialized Space: Obama and the Rhetorical Constraints of Phenotypical Blackness" Facilitator: 2. Bring response to the reading for the week that you found the most provocative
Week 4 *Defining haunting whiteness; color blindness; hauntings in social media*	1. Prior to class, have read the following in *Rhetorics of Whiteness*: – Foreword and Introduction. Reflection to Part Two (by Catherine Prendergast) – "Racialized Slacktivism: Social Media Performances of White Antiracism" Facilitator: – "The Ghost's in the Machine: eHarmony and the Reification of Whiteness and Heteronormativity" Facilitator:	1. Prior to class, have read the following: – "Facebook and Absent-Present Rhetorics of Whiteness" Facilitator: – "Color-Blind Rhetoric in Obama's 2008 'Race Speech'" Facilitator: 2. Discuss book review as a genre: aims, audiences, and conventions.
Week 5 *Book reviews*	Reading day for book reviews	In-class short oral presentations about the books you've read.

(*cont.*)

TABLE 5.1   Weekly agenda (cont.)

Week	Day 1	Day 2
Week 6 *Memoir and dialogues*	1. Polished written version of *book review* due. 2. Prior to class, have read, the two sample memoirs in this book.	Prior to class, have read the two sample critical dialogues in this book.
Week 7 *Defining and defying stereotypes of poor whites*	Prior to class, have read the following in *White Trash: Race and Class in America*: – Introduction by Annalee Newitz and Matt Wray – John H. Hartigan Jr.'s "Objectifying 'Poor Whites' and 'White Trash' in Detroit" Facilitator: – Roxanne Dunbar's "Bloody Footprints: Reflections on Growing up Poor White" Facilitator:	1. Prior to class, have read: – "White Trash Religion" Facilitator: – bell hooks "Madonna: Plantation Mistress or Soul Sister." 2. Bring response to hooks.
Week 8 *Whiteness: Culture's Role*	Prior to class, watch CNN video about Santa and Jesus and have read the following from *Critical White Studies*: – "Do You Know This Man?" and "The Curse of Ham" Facilitator: – "White Innocence, Black Abstraction" and "On the Making of Invisible People" Facilitator:	Prior to class, have read the following from *Rhetorics of Whiteness*: – "*The Help* as Noncomplicit Identification and Nostalgic Revision" Facilitator: – "Must(n't) See TV: Hidden Whiteness in Representation of Women of Color" Facilitator:

(*cont.*)

TABLE 5.1 Weekly agenda (cont.)

Week	Day 1	Day 2
Week 9 *Satire, Research Comedy, and Critiquing Whiteness*	Prior to class, watch the following videos: Adam Ruins Everything "The Disturbing History of the Suburbs" and John Oliver's "Trump's Wall."	*Memoir/Dialogue due beginning of class*
Week 10 *Hauntings in Education and Culture*	Prior to class, have read the following in *Rhetorics of Whiteness*: – "Washing Education White" Facilitator: – "How Whiteness Haunts the Textbook Industry" Facilitator:	Peer review of Memoir/Dialogue; bring 3 full-draft copies.
Week 11 *Hauntings in Pedagogy*	Prior to class, have read the following in *Rhetorics of Whiteness*: – "On the Cover of the Rolling Stones: Deconstructing Monsters and Terrorism in an Era of Postracial Whiteness" Collaborative Facilitators: – "The Pedagogical Role of a White Instructor's Racial Awareness Narrative" Collaborative Facilitators:	1. Prior to class, have read the following: – "Practicing Mindfulness: A Pedagogical Tool for Spotlighting Whiteness" Collaborative Facilitators: – Amy Winans' "Cultivating Racial Literacy in White, Segregated Settings: Emotions as Site of Ethical Engagement and Inquiry" Collaborative Facilitators: 2. Bring response discussing the role of whiteness in your own education.

(cont.)

TABLE 5.1 Weekly agenda (*cont.*)

Week	Day 1	Day 2
Week 12 *Producing and Consuming Whiteness*	Prior to class, have the following from *Critical Whiteness Studies*: – "Race and the Dominant Gaze: Narratives of Law and Inequality in Popular Film" Collaborative Facilitators: – "The Other Pleasures: The Narrative Function of Race in Cinema" Collaborative Facilitators:	1. From *Rhetorics of Whiteness*: "Color Deafness: White Writing as Palimpsest for African American English in *Breaking Bad* Screen Captioning and Video Technologies" Collaborative Facilitators: 2. Discuss Cultural Studies Analysis; examine sample.
Week 13 *Reconstructing Race Relations in/for the Twenty-First Century: Our Roles as Anti-Racist Rhetoricians. Race Traitors. Allies.*	Activity/readings related to allyship to be announced. Collaborative Facilitators:	Response topic to be announced.
Week 14 *Reflect/wrap up the semester*	*Peer review of cultural studies rhetorical analysis*; bring 3 full-draft copies. Optional conferences.	Final class reflections.
Week 15 *Finishing touches*		Submit cultural studies analysis.

CHAPTER 6

Sample Assignments with Sample Student Texts

1   Considerations for Writing Short Responses

1. Responses to readings: These are 3 typed paragraphs, spaces for you to enter into a dialogue with an author about one or two related ideas/issues raised in the piece.
2. For the first paragraph, provide a paragraph summarizing one or two key points you feel merit close attention.
3. Next, provide an analysis paragraph, focusing on one or two aspects of *how* the piece is written, paying particular attention to the author's use of various rhetorical appeals or other strategies. How does the author construct (or damage) her ethos? How does the author make use of personal narrative, statistics, references to other thinkers, etc.? Point to specific moments in the texts—perhaps, even quoting—to back up your points.
4. Finally, respond by entering into a dialogue with the text: where do you agree, disagree, get annoyed, get excited? Back up your points with textual references and with references to your own lived experiences or to current events.
5. Format: Use MLA format—double-spaced, typed, 10–12 pt font, header, etc.
6. General considerations:
   – Introduction—Begin by introducing the author and title of piece to which you are responding, followed by a quote or brief paraphrase of the idea to which you are responding (with a corresponding in-text parenthetical page citation—so that your readers know from which pages the specific ideas are taken). Then, move onto responding to those ideas.
   – Move from General to the Specific (avoid merely stating vague generalizations)

1.1   *Grading*
– An *A* response: Is clearly focused around one or two related ideas that the author of the piece actually brought up; paraphrases or quotes directly those ideas with page references. Goes beyond the obvious, and really adds something to the conversation or helps clarify or work out an idea for yourself and your classmates. Moves beyond the realm of the vague or abstract

to concretize ideas through illustrations, anecdotes, specific examples, observations, etc. Has at least 3 well-developed paragraphs. Potentially grapples with a complex idea, even admitting ambiguity, but not necessarily coming up with a quick or overly simplified answer.
- A *B* response: Is focused around one or two related ideas that could be more clearly articulated or developed. One paragraph may be weaker than the other two. Provides some illustrations, but paragraphs/ideas could use a bit more clarification or support.
- A *B-/C+* response: Is rather short, general, and/or underdeveloped but does indicate the writer read the piece but, perhaps, tries to discuss too many subtopics so that no single topic is developed. Needs a bit more clarification for rhetorical points. Tends to remain more in the vague or abstract, rather than providing clarification for ideas raised. Is closer to 1 page in length.
- A *C/C-* response: Indicates the writer read the piece but doesn't do much more. Closer to a summary than a dialogic response.
- A *D-F* response: Speaks on the general topic but gives no evidence the writer actually read the piece, or the writer seems to have misunderstood the author's argument.

2   Sample Response

By Abby Graves

The chapter, "Madonna: Plantation Mistress of Soul Sister," written by bell hooks in *Black on White: Black Writers on What it Means to Be White*, analyzes the problematic nature of Madonna's stage persona, including both the personality traits she embodies, and those with whom she interacts—or more accurately—whom she dominates. The primary argument hooks presents involves the exposure of Madonna's exploitation of "black" qualities. For instance, black women are condemned for having "sexual agency and transgression," while Madonna, exhibiting those very quality, is praised a rebellious, progressive white girl (310). As well, even though Madonna admits she puts much effort into her performative appearance, she nevertheless emulates a hyper-exaggerated "pure" white woman; she "mocks the conventional racist defined beauty ideal even as she rigorously strives to embody it" (309). These stereotypical "black" qualities presents Madonna as exotic and rebellious, where on black stars, they are detrimental to their character. The second main point hooks discusses is Madonna's "fascistic" domination over oppressed people, and exploitation of them under the guise of being liberating. Though having a large drag and gay following, Madonna portrays people gay people as "emotionally handicapped or defective" in order to exact her domination over them (315). Madonna also presents black people as caricatures— black women as "mammies," and black men as "phallic black masculinity," using them as a tool to compete with white masculinity. Madonna's oppressive portrayals "mock and undermine" black qualities so that she can "upstage" them, upholding Madonna's white power, in comparison (311). While claiming to be a powerful feminist figure, she simply reproduces the patriarchy in "the same old phallic nonsense with white pussy at the center," while "her exaggerated whiteness allows her to stay innocent," unlike the underprivileged people from who she borrows, who are demonized if they act a certain way, or display a certain quality that white society deems a stereotype (315).

Though the piece is a critical analysis of a popular figure and its racial and patriarchal implications, hooks uses her own voice, colloquial terms, and personal anecdotes to qualify her claims as what they are: her own opinions. For instance, hooks describes Shirley Temple's interaction with the offensively, stereotypically exaggerated black character, Bojangles, and that, in comparison, the audience was not supposed to see black people as people, but rather as a tool, for white people "to see what a special little old white girl Shirley was" (313). The description, "what a special little old white girl" is a colloquial exclamation (i.e., "what a sweet girl!") as in, though structured as a question, the speaker is expressing her shock and overwhelming emotion in reaction to the situation, as if the speaker is not even able to fully comprehend it. In a sarcastic manner, hooks employs this wording style to ironically make the claim that white people are exploiting black people in order to uplift themselves even further to show her insincerity, and thus rejection, to the claim that Shirley truly is such "a special little old white girl." Also, hooks directly states when she uses personal experiences, and when she inserts personal anecdotes. Once, hooks says, she was "joking about the film with other black folks, [and] we commented that Madonna must have searched long and hard to find a black female that was not a good dancer..." (314). Additionally, hooks identifies clearly when her opinions are personal and subjective to her, such as when she states, "I can only say this doesn't sound like liberation to me" (315), and, "I was angered by her visual domination over...people of color and white working-class women...I was too angered...to appreciate other aspects of the film I might have enjoyed" (313). The use of first person and direct identification of the self, her black self, is to hooks' advantage in her argument of oppression and exploitation of black people. The ethos of a black woman, as well as direct admission of a personal statement, rather than a blanket generalization, directly addresses areas where she is biased or opinionated, which protects her from much possible counterargument. By admitting her biases, and with her true anecdotal experiences of being oppressed, from the perspective of a black female, this allows her argument to maintain its strength, as she is speaking as the object or racism, rather than an outside voyeur simply commenting on the power structure.

I find hooks' piece to be compelling, and especially relevant, within the subtopic of using oppressed minority subgroups to the advantage of an oppressor or oppressive systems, such as current marketing within advertising, tokenization in companies for the appearance of diversity, or, in this case, to uphold Madonna's status as a rebellious white girl who "likes to play mother" to disadvantaged people as a means of gaining fame and power (315). Many companies, now that social justice has become a popular issue in politics, have begun to use this new focus to sell products by stamping a photo of a diverse group of friends enjoying their branded beverage or changing their logo to a Pride flag (only for the duration of Pride month, however). Madonna not only uses images of gay, drag, and black culture to sell herself as a performer, but goes further, and also embodies those images, and thus, appropriates them. Madonna rips these qualities from their context, not giving due credit, and shamelessly using them to create her own "bad" white girl image—something for which black people themselves are shamed if they do. As in advertisements, Madonna uses oppressed people as props. For instance, "Madonna almost always imitates phallic black masculinity," such as in her choreographed "crotch-grabbing [scandal which was] and eloquent put-down of male phallic pride—" *black* pride, specifically (311). Madonna uses this phallic black imagery, not because she actually cares about helping oppressed black people, but so that her image is deemed as dangerous, worldly, cultural, powerful, ultimately in competition with white patriarchal systems, just as all other guises of social justice in "every other group of white supremacist society" do (311). Though Madonna claims to be a powerful feminist with good intentions for her diverse and much oppressed audience, she nevertheless contributes to oppressive systems by using black people, working women, and LGBTQ people as props and as means to her own fame, extorting and manipulating them as she pleases, then claiming that is what those people need, or even want. After reading and considering hooks' analysis, I now watch such videos with a more skeptical, analytical eye.

3 Facilitation Guidelines

In keeping with the seminar format, in which all participants (students and professor, alike) engage the seminar's focus with rigor and enthusiasm, each seminar participant will help lead our discussion for two of our readings this semester. Each facilitation should last 15–20 minutes (undergrads)/20–25 minutes (grads) and must include at least one relevant visual: a handout with quotes and questions, a visual from the web, an overhead, etc. You may also include an activity to engage different discussion styles: reflective writing; debating; charting/mapping; dividing us into small groups to tease out, role play, or illustrate an idea or quote, etc. You may include a relevant video, but no more than 5 minutes of it.

The idea is to engage with the assigned reading by doing at least 2 of the following (for undergraduate students) or 3 of the following (graduate students):
– *Teasing out nuances* in the author's argument or perspective (not simply summarizing).
– *Complicating* the author's ideas with references to other texts, statistics, local situations, and so on.
– *Synthesizing* the perspectives of the author with those presented in other texts (in the course or beyond).
– Relating the reading's ideas to *current events*.
– Exploring an author's use of *rhetorical strategies*.

Your facilitation will be our primary time with each reading, so it is important that you do an excellent job of addressing pertinent issues raised in a particular reading. Please keep us active and engaged by having a plan and preparing well. Remember, you are not lecturing or summarizing the entire text. Feel free to briefly summarize a particular issue and/or to point us to specific passages under discussion. Make efforts to draw others in and to keep the discussion productive.

[Be sure to avoid the, "Okay, so what did you all think?" approach—which implies a lack of preparation or forethought. If you are struggling for ideas, make an appointment with the professor.]

3.1 *Grading*

A range: Facilitation evidences a high degree of planning or creativity and really engages participants in a thoughtful activity/discussion that provides us with new insights, helps us relate ideas beyond the reading, or helps us puzzle out tough questions. All participants are engaged. Facilitator keeps discussion productively focused and draws out participants. Visuals are relevant, aesthetically appealing, and accessible (not boring, too small to read, too cramped, etc.). Time is managed wisely.

B range: Facilitation evidences pre-planning and some creativity and engages most participants in an activity/discussion that helps us better understand the material and relate it beyond the reading. Visuals/activities are engaging but could use some refining. Facilitator, perhaps, summarizes too much or could manage time more wisely.

C to D range: Facilitator clearly read the reading but doesn't seem to have put much effort into planning for the facilitation. Participants lack engagement or fail to come to much insight beyond a basic understanding of ideas presented in the text. Videos or visuals are poorly introduced or made use of. No actual references are made to direct quotes so that participants talk in general, rather than in dialogue with the text.

4   Book Review Assignment

Length: 2.5–4 pp. single-spaced, typed
Audience: Participants in our seminar (Academic Audience)
Due: Present verbally in class
Due: Post polished written version as attachment in Discussion Board

You will each read and present a review of a full-length book that addresses whiteness. The purpose of the review is both to encourage you to read an intellectual discussion by a scholar of whiteness studies and to educate the rest of us about what kind of work in this area is out there; these reviews allow us as a class wider exposure to the larger conversation than we each could read individually. Remember that the review is not merely a summary, but a critical analysis of the author's central arguments, as well as a commentary about the efficacy of the discussion and potential audiences for the book.

Format: Follow standard book review format: see example in Canvas for listing the book title, author, publication information, etc. Type your text in 10–12 pt font in an accessible font. List your name and university affiliation at the end of the review. Use block format for paragraphs: do not indent; instead double space between paragraphs.

Introduction: Take the first paragraph to introduce the book title and author and to introduce your audience to the context of the book: was it a study? What genre is the book? What is the main premise/argument of the text? Note: when you first reference the author, do so by the full name listed on the title page: Elizabeth A. Banks. After that, refer to the author by last name or by "the author." Never refer to an author you do not personally know by first name. Bring the author's name back in throughout your review to help your audience remember that these are not your ideas.

Summary: Take the next few paragraphs to overview the main arguments forwarded in the text. Be sure to differentiate between outlining and summarizing. That is, do not simply say what the author talks about; instead, summarize the main points she is making. Paraphrase as much as possible, and quote sparingly. When you do quote, be sure to follow MLA format for quoting. Always lead into quotes with a signal phrase, and be sure to provide a parenthetical page reference after the quote.

Conclude: In your concluding section/s, you get to add in your two cents, your evaluation of the book. Who are the best audiences for the book? What are the book's strengths/weaknesses? Was there anything you wish the author had covered more thoroughly? Is the book dense? Very readable? What of the author's style do you want to note for your readers?

Citations: If you cite any other sources besides the primary text you are reviewing, be sure to include a Works Cited at the end of your text.

In-Class Presentation: Take 5 minutes to verbally review your book for us. Tell us the title, author, and main premise. You don't have to be as thorough as you are in your written review. Be sure to take a couple of minutes to invite and field questions from your audience.

Evaluation: Your review will be evaluated on how accurately you present the author's main arguments, on how well you introduced the book and its context, on your critique of the book, and on your professional voice as an academic writer. Be sure to take time to proofread for grammar and sentence structure. Be sure to edit your prose: cut redundancy, edit clunky wording, and check for transitions within and between paragraphs.

5   Sample Book Review

Not Quite White: White Trash and the Boundaries of Whiteness
Matt Wray
Duke University Press, 2006, 213 pp.
ISBN 9780822338826

In *Not Quite White: White Trash and the Boundaries of Whiteness,* Matt Wray narrows in on the notion of *poor white trash* to question the boundaries and limitations of whiteness as a paradigm of inequality. Wray describes the term as a caste of rural Americans that attracted disdain from a number of social groups, most notably socially dominant, affluent whites. Wray devotes his book to examining how a series of derogatory terms for a group of poor whites blur the seemingly clear social lines of demarcation between whites and nonwhites. Largely a case study on the historical impact of the term *white trash* and its boundaries in the United States, Wray's argument is twofold: it rests upon an exhortation to move beyond *white trash's* simplicity and condescension, and into an understanding of the term's use as a label, stigma, and stereotype—in other words, to conceive whiteness as a term of racial domination proves limiting. Second, Wray urges his readers to consider inequalities of race, gender, sexuality, and class as a series of related sub processes that contribute to a larger process of social differentiation, rather than distinct, autonomous processes (1, 5). Wray's thoughtful approach is interdisciplinary; he blends historical analysis and boundary theory with whiteness and social studies by analyzing literature, journalism, historical writings, scientific and medical writing, and social sciences. The author uses primary texts to show that *poor white trash*, though originating in the American South, was applied broadly to whites who were seen as poor, lazy, and immoral—un-white, as it were. In its broader context, Wray calls for a new proposal on whiteness studies: to be reconceptualized as a flexible set of social and symbolic boundaries (6).

Wray devotes space up front to outline the various theoretical underpinnings behind his argument. The author explores concepts such as boundary theory and whiteness studies, situating his argument within a larger—and more academic—context. Wray uses boundary theory, the notion that social and symbolic boundaries are an inescapable aspect of the human experience (9), as a framework through which to analyze the plight of those viewed as *poor white trash*. Thus, boundary theory becomes the linchpin of his argument. Wray notes: "making and marking group boundaries as processes deeply rooted in both our individual and collective consciousness... the situation of poor whites has always been one of ambiguity and liminality, attributes shared by the identity—white trash—so frequently ascribed to them" (16–17).

Throughout the study, Wray traces the various slurs and *stigmatyping* (a word Wray coins) terms as they pertain to larger themes of social perceptions health, wealth, location, and immorality. The author's argument about *white trash* is focused around a few central notions that differentiate marginalized whites from other castes. These boundary terms shirk traditional notions of race, gender, and status as the sole processes for social differentiation. In the opening sections of *Not Quite White* the author introduces such terms as *lubber* and *cracker*, showing how the terms set the stage for the concept of *poor white trash*. The trajectory of *lubbers* and *crackers* stigmatizes those to whom the modifiers are attributed as the "other." "Othering" poor whites place them in contradiction to the colonial goal of morality and industriousness through hard work, an idea promoted by prominent settlers like William Byrd II, to whom Wray devotes significant attention. Thus, *lubbers*, who were rendered useless and pushed to the colonial frontier due to free white labor were seen as "non-white," as they—literally—lived among natives on the frontier. In *cracker*, some advances were made: marginalized whites were no longer seen as lazy, as were *lubbers*, but dangerous, treacherous, and arrogant. A distinction then forms between *cracker* and *dirt-eater*, a group whose perceived physical deformities, laziness, and low intelligence were influenced by their diet. In the case of the latter group, the term *dirt-eaters* was disseminated to a broader audience via comedy, becoming a popular put down. Ultimately, Wray settles into *white trash* as the predominant term, noting its origin in black slave rhetoric; the author thus spends ample time examining the term's rhetorical power. Wray is careful to note throughout that with *poor white trash*, the issue is not one of delineation between races, as much as within race.

To advance his theories, *Not Quite White* employs what Wray terms a "historical interactionist" (16) approach to the case study of poor whites, wherein he examines a 200-year period in America, from the British colonies of the 1720s, to the Reconstruction period of the 1920s, through analyzing primary texts and scholarly sources. Wray creates a quasi-linear historical narrative in *Not Quite White;* each chapter traces and documents various social interactions between whites, Native Americans, black slaves, and poor, rural whites. Wray draws from an array of texts from each period, refusing to focus solely on sources from any one class or racial group. He also provides evidence from alternate stances, such as the abolitionist rhetoric of Harriet Beecher Stowe, that attempt to "rescue" whites from such stigmatized language as *white trash, dirt eater, lubber,* or *cracker.*

As *white trash* assimilated into American vernacular as a term declaring poor white's marginal status and low foothold on the social hierarchies of the antebellum, Civil War, and Reconstruction social climates, efforts to rescue whites from being deemed morally inferior were proposed. By this point, *poor white trash* had most notably rooted itself in the South. Wray outlines this battle in terms of abolitionist rhetoric—promulgated by Harriet Beecher Stowe—which argued that slavery is the reason for the condition of the poor white by way of being cheated out of land, gospel, and labor, and secessionist rhetoric, which argued "bad blood" was the generating cause of the *poor white trash*, not social or political circumstances. Thus, the poor white problem, so to speak, of the South and U.S. is the problem of sexual degeneracy. Wray notes that this rhetoric led to the problematic rise of eugenics, within which feeblemindedness was attached to morality. Enter hookworm. Wray shows that medical examinations of hookworm could account for a majority of the *stimgatyped* rhetoric surrounding poor whites. In a clear linear cause and effect chain, Wray elucidates the argument: dirt eater = hookworm = feeblemindedness and idiocy, which leads to moral corruption. Therefore, to improve physical health was to return poor whites to being useful, normalized white behavior, "opening the door for moral uplift, economic rebirth, and civic renewal" (118).

Wray's audience exists somewhere in between strictly academic and general. Though he peppers in theoretical notions, such as Marxist theories and Kantian "schema," the book reads relatively easily; in fact, most of Wray's academic discourse is treated in a series of lengthy endnotes; in the endnotes, which are sometimes a page or more themselves, Wray extends the conversation, bolstering claims with references and providing more academic context. Wray deserves praise for his nuanced argument: it weaves a complex narrative that problematizes stigmas against poor whites. *Not Quite White* rejects nativism as a determining factor of the poor white (81), as Wray chocks the liminal status of the poor white to a series of blurred boundary terms and social distinctions. Ultimately—and the author notes this—much of the research and conclusions remain open ended and inconclusive, a strong and admirable foray into a new area of study on white trash. Wray charts out a path, but only accompanies us along the first few steps. Some of this is the nature of the subject: whiteness studies are still evolving, the clean narrative of the study can cause the careful reader to be cautious, and *white trash* remains a popular slur for the marginalized white, generally depicted as Southern, seen as poor, dim, or sexually immoral (think of the incest comments). Nevertheless, Wray's agenda is admirable and his research is, without doubt, meticulous. This book is valuable contribution to those interested in, or studying, marginalized whites.

Thomas Drake Farmer, The University of Tennessee at Chattanooga

6   Sample Review of Book Read in Electronic Format

White Fragility: Why It's So Hard for White People to Talk about Racism
Robin DiAngelo
E-Book, Beacon Press, 2018. 169 pp.
ISBN 9780807047415

Robin DiAngelo leads a provocative unmasking of white perspective, superiority and entitlement in her book, *White Fragility: Why It's So Hard for White People to Talk About Racism,* trudging deep into the social, ideological contradictions that protect white dominance: dominance in a country that espouses ideals about freedom, opportunity, and equality. DiAngelo draws from her many years as a Diversity Trainer, where she has been placed to intervene in the lives of her fellow whites to address implicit racism, often with disastrous results. The book is nonfiction dissemination of white sociology. Her thesis is that white people have been raised in racial isolation and ignorance, which results in a lack of emotional stability to deal with conversations about racism in a mature way. DiAngelo uses her experiences as evidence that white people are fragile and often argue, withdraw, or cry to shove off any hint of being called racist. DiAngelo's purpose is not to just prove that White Fragility exists, but to reveal the pillars of racism that cause it and to convince her fellow whites to combat it.

The author begins her book by claiming a truer definition of racism, which she defines as a social and institutional dominance that floods into every facet of society. She asserts that it is an omnipresent ocean of biases, ideologies, and systems we all swim through and absorb. She explains that every position of power in America is dominated by white folk (d. 2, tr. 5, 3:55–5:07), and therefore, every law, curriculum, and product released in America is skewed by the white perspective, racist messages, representations and cultural biases, or as DiAngelo borrows the term from Sociologist Joe Feagin, "The White Frame" (d. 2, tr. 7, 3:39–4:53). In chapter one, she stresses how we are taught to see things through the lens of the American ideologies of individualism and objectivity (d. 1, tr. 8, 1:07–1:34), both of which are far from true. The author describes The White Frame as a perspective we are all taught to look through, which decides what is important and what is not. It is not decided consciously by us or objectively through reason. Instead, it is a byproduct of our upbringing and our interactions with other people and with mainstream media. This is what DiAngelo calls "Socialization" (d. 1, tr. 8, 2:53–4:56), and it is proof that the American ideals of individual success and objective reasoning are just as fragile as whites. DiAngelo claims that this mistaken faith in human objectivity pushes the idea of implicit bias and unconscious racism from the white mind, making constructive talk of racism impossible, because the only possible racism in that mindset is conscious, and since a white person never chose to be racist, they must not be racist (d. 1, tr. 5, 2:09–2:26). The result of this idea and the previous ideologies is that white people feel personally attacked as if they had been accused of murder when someone gives them feedback on their racist stereotypes (d. 3, tr. 9, 2:26–3:59). This is a prime example of what DiAngelo refers to as White Fragility.

From here, DiAngelo picks up her narrative by addressing all the ways white people are given unearned privilege and are complicit in that advantage. She gives examples of freedom from responsibility (d. 2, tr. 18, 1:18–1:48) and transparency (d. 2, tr. 1, 4:41–5:13), which highlight how white is the default setting. How white is considered not raced, which exempts white people from having to bear a responsibility to their race. The author asserts that white people do not feel the need to educate themselves about their race and the races of others. Whites have the freedom to be ignorant. Second, DiAngelo points to White Solidarity, the concept of whites enjoying their status as part of the superior in-group (d. 3, tr. 2, 0:00–0:40). The educated can laugh at the uneducated, a sneer which is validated by whites' mistaken belief in individuality, that all people have equal access to success and they just have to work hard enough to get there. Whites can confide in the dangers of "urban neighborhoods," which is coded language for "black neighborhoods" (d. 2, tr. 13, 0:43–1:32), a racist stereotype we can deny if it is ever brought up. The author goes on to stress how anti-black these conversations are, but they don't seem anti-black because the participants use coded language and point to specific attributes such as safety and education without explicitly naming blacks. A rule of White Solidarity is that the conversation must never consider *why* black neighborhoods are stereotypically considered more dangerous when, as DiAngelo stresses, there is more danger to people of color in white neighborhoods than to white people in black neighborhoods (d. 2, tr. 14, 4:33–4:53; d. 3, tr. 4, 1:31–1:38). These kinds of coded conversations breed not just solidarity and an us-and-them mentality, but also a feeling of superiority. According to DiAngelo, the loss of that superiority when the in-group steps out of line shakes the elevated comradery of white civilization and drives whites into outbursts of White Fragility.

White Fragility, as DiAngelo defines it, is the by-product of white superiority, white solidarity, individualism, objectivity and ideals of equality against the backdrop of rampant segregation. It is usually expressed in outrage, tears, or retreating from the conversation. The white person makes a scenario where the topic moves from racism to how hard the white person's life is (d. 4, tr. 12, 4:35–5:21; d. 4, tr. 13, 0:00–0:21; d. 4, tr. 16, 0:56–1:43), or how difficult it is to get a job, or how the giver of the feedback is victimizing the white person according to some other form of bias, or how their feelings had been hurt. All of these push the conversation away from constructive feedback about racism and so maintain white dominance. DiAngelo posits that white dominance is so prevalent because it is so vehemently defended. She stresses how when white people are fragile, it is because they are uncomfortable, not because they are in any danger (d. 5, tr. 1, 3:15–3:23; d. 5, tr. 9, 1:40–1:58). As a member of the dominant group, they do not have to fear persecution, being fired, or being murdered on account of racism. This illuminates the greatest irony: how in the face of America's history, continual segregation and the American dream of equality, white people ignore history, feel safe in segregated communities, and are willing to put people of color down and shy away from conversations that promote equality for the sake of their comfort. That is White Fragility.

After demonstrating White Fragility's existence and its impact, DiAngelo frames the last section of her book on how to combat White Fragility. Her guiding idea in this section is the subject of Racial Stamina, the opposite of White Fragility. Racial Stamina is the ability to live with being uncomfortable and taking feedback gratefully (d. 1, tr. 3, 4:14–4:23). The author points out that anyone giving feedback knows how awkward the subject matter is, and that the person receiving it is unlikely to accept it. This means that any feedback is a show of trust (d. 5, tr. 9, 1:11–1:21). DiAngelo encourages whites to consider overcoming their socialization into racism as a matter of life-or-death. Further, she encourages whites to do their homework, to not shove the responsibility of education on their friends who are people of color, and to be grateful for every piece of feedback they get (d. 5, tr. 2, 1:13–1:19). The author reminds her audience that no one chose to be socialized into whiteness, but we do choose our participation in it.

This book is a deep look into a uniquely white idea: how intellectual fragility can reinforce and preserve a dominant group's position. Because it is clearly written for white people, the author employs rhetorical strategies that ease her audience into the idea that everyone holds racist biases. For instance, DiAngelo uses the "we" more than "I" or "you" to build her ethos as a white person. Her experience in dealing with white people is apparent from how comprehensively she can foresee and address objections. This is a major advantage in prompting whites to be honest about their biases, and it keeps audiences engaged. Diplomatic phrasing and examples of insensitivity by white people are built to keep white readers from dismissing the book's content. Of course, throughout the entire book, DiAngelo is calling her audience racist. She works to redefine racism throughout the narrative but cannot fully anticipate how audiences will receive this accusation. The subject is confined by the language of today, in which ordinary citizens do not tend to have the vocabulary to parse between racist extremism and socialization into a racist culture. Furthermore, because her book cannot cover racism in every sense, DiAngelo admits the need for readers to get more involved in learning about racism (d. 5, tr. 14, 3:31–3:57). The full bed of evidence this book offers is first-hand accounts, which are not convincing in representing all white people; however, I do not think this detracts from the book. The point of the book is to prompt white people to look inward on themselves, not outward to the whole of America. Solving White Fragility starts with the one person you can control: yourself. Robin DiAngelo didn't write *White Fragility* solely to prove that White Fragility exists. She wrote it to encourage each reader, individually, to take up the responsibility of combatting it, and through my own reading of it, I believe, and hope, that she succeeded.

Connor McPherson, *The University of Tennessee at Chattanooga*

7   Memoir or Critical Dialogue

Length: 6–8 pp. undergrads; 8–10 pp. grads

For this assignment, you may either compose a memoir exploring your own encounter or experience with race (being read as white; being privileged as white; reading others as white; encountering white privilege in others; mistrusting someone due to their perceived race, etc.) OR create a dialogue between the writer-thinkers we will read this semester.

For the memoir: Situate/position/narrate yourself as a person with a particular racial history and experience; explore moments of concord/dissonance/

rupture in your encounters with self or others as beings constructed racially. Remember, a memoir is different from an expository essay in that you narrate, rather than explain or argue. You want to show, rather than tell: to do so, include dialogue, action, conflict, sensory imagery and concrete detail. Set the scene. As we discussed in class, you do not need to follow chronological order; sometimes, it works well to begin in the middle of things or to have flashbacks. If you do follow chronological order, be sure to avoid list-like prose. Try to write for a specific audience/publication, and feel free to design your text as it would actually appear (using columns, headers, pull quotes, color, photos, art, etc. to draw in reader interest and enhance content). Note: if you choose this option, you'll need to seriously think about your own racial positioning/affiliations/predicaments, etc., so be prepared to take the risks of self-examination and exposure that accompany memoir.

For the dialogue: Choose a theme or topic to serve as a focus, select three or four voices from our readings that represent a range of perspectives on/approaches to whiteness, and compose a well-crafted conversation between them. Each "character" in your dialogue should speak for at least a paragraph or two each time he/she speaks and should speak at least twice. If you alter a speaker's actual words to make the conversation flow, be sure to stay true to the person's character and to note your alterations through the use of [brackets]. Each speaker should treat the other's perspective seriously, if skeptically, but with respect. Do not simply ping pong between speakers. Try to find actual connections in what speakers are saying. Enter the dialogue yourself as a moderator, but also as a speaker. You are striving for a thoughtful, balanced treatment/synthesis of the topic or issue in question. Be sure to introduce/set up the dialogue, however you've constructed it: a talk show, an online dialogue, a town hall meeting, etc. Be sure to include a Works Cited and in-text, cite the pages from which you are drawing the quotes.

Writer's Statement
- For the memoir, include a brief statement (one paragraph) about the intended audience/publication for the piece. Would it appear in a specific magazine or journal? What ages, genders, regions, etc. are you most trying to reach?
- For the dialogue, include your introductory statement in the actual dialogue (see examples we've looked at) so that you are introducing your audience to what's up with the dialogue. Take time to introduce speakers and their credentials and introduce your audience to the focused topic for discussion.

Title: Give your memoir or your dialogue an engaging title.

8   Sample Memoir

I Am (Not) Your Gringo
by Daniel Giraldo

> "Borders are set up to define the places that are safe and unsafe, to distinguish us from them. A border is a dividing line, a narrow strip along a steep edge. A borderland is a vague and undetermined place created by the emotional residue of an unnatural boundary."
>
> GLORIA ANZALDÚA

• • •

"¿Y el que tiene de Latino?" my grandmother asked my grandfather in an unconcerned tone. Her head, along with the end of her fork, gestured in my direction.

We had finished *el almuerzo* and, as was typical of a midday meal on the farm, the three of us saved room for *sobremesa*. Most times there was already a Ziploc baggie on the table full of some delicacy they'd saved from recent travels. In this case, though, we topped off our stomachs with *avena*—a sweetened, silky, stewed-oatmeal drink: imagine having a whole glass full of that last sip drained from a bowl of Cinnamon Toast Crunch. It'd been tenderly prepared from a gallon of extra *leche* brought over by the closest neighbor, Jesse. But after hearing my grandmother's question, what would have been a treat to my taste buds instead turned sour in my mouth.

The words she spoke were her response to my grandfather's statement of caution, made in light of recent events, warning me to keep a low profile. Talk of deportation and a wall along the border with Mexico seemed to have summoned up within him a mild case of hate-crime paranoia. He'd known (and witnessed) discrimination before, he said, having lived and labored in St. Bernard Parish, in pre-Katrina New Orleans, Louisiana. Wave after wave of social inequality had eroded his sense of security long before the deluge came to claim his home. Now, my grandfather felt it was his duty to prepare me for the worst. He pointed out how unsafe it was to be among the minority, a Latino in the South.

But like my grandmother's question implied, I had no reason to be concerned for my safety. In fact, I wasn't the least bit bothered by what worried my grandfather. His were not the words that slithered surreptitiously along the grassy edge of my mind.

My grandmother had a point, I guess, by asking exactly what could possibly give my ethnicity away. Her words; however, had caught me off guard. They'd caused me to trip over something unexpected—something that had long been repressed—something hidden from view. It had nothing to do with the causes and effects of racism. No, it had everything to do with a selfish justification that I am who I thought I was.

What is it that makes me Latino, I've often wondered to myself. Surely, the physical markers cannot be all that obscured. My eyes were like their eyes. I also wore with pride my darkened hair. My nose was wide in comparison to my Tennessean peers. It stood out as a testament to my South American roots. Then again, I know it's not so much about what can be seen by *el ojo desnudo*.

"Pues la sangre la tiene el," my grandfather replied in my defense. He seemed somewhat astonished at the question posed by his wife.

For my grandfather, ethnicity seemed to be something that was passed down through generations. It's as encoded into biological heritage as are genetic heirlooms sequenced into the fig trees planted outside their home. Mine was stored in blood, he'd said, the proof being somewhere buried deep within a double-helix pudding.

Wherever my ethnicity was, however, it'd lain dormant year after year. Or perhaps it was just in the weeds, waiting to be discovered. Like a surprise vine of cucumbers that's been twisting all along beneath tall grass, they're never quite like what's expected. They're different than the variety planted a season or two ago. They've blanched; not from over-exposure to the sun, but because they'd been covered up completely by their environment. Grass and fallen leaves.

Cucumbers need sunlight to develop and maintain their traditionally green color, to stay true to their roots. But I was akin to their paler cousins, I'd thought. I'd drawn the parallel while preparing the soil for planting, after lunch that day on the farm.

It's not that I've ever doubted my lineage—my parents are both from Colombia, South America, after all. I've just never been able to fully accept it. Not even after traveling there several times over the years. And not even because of comments like the one made by my grandmother over lunch that day.

There's always been another barrier blocking me from mainly identifying as who I feel I am, to feeling connected to the rhizomatic plateaus defined as family. I knew what my grandmother meant by her question, at the table, on the farm, and it was not at all like what I'd felt others in my family had meant before. For them, I suppose, it was my lack of skill in Spanish that'd forever make me *gringo*. For me, it was what this word meant, and all its bodily implications, that'd always made me feel inadequately enculturated.

• • •

The first time I'd heard the word *gringo* was after it had already been said countless times before. It only ever sunk in because it'd finally been applied to me.

A faulty conjugation would give way to harmless teasing. Perhaps it was my stubborn tongue that couldn't roll a proper *r*? Whatever the reason might have been, being called a *gringo* (as a Latino) made me feel slow, like I was *caído del zarzo*, or something. I was different from even my family, each of whom had probably never been called a *gringo* ever before in their lives. And I felt this way all because of language.

Growing up in Tennessee, *gringo* was a term typically used by someone who looked browner than me for someone who wasn't. The fact that I'd been called a *gringo* by my own kin wasn't that big of a deal, I guess, but until now it'd disrupted my ability to process who I am. While it's mainly used to describe a non-Spanish speaking North American of any color, any inflection can contain every negative connotation that being from this side of the U.S. border brings—mainly ignorance or just plain stupidity.

For me, I had associated the word with the latter, and having been raised in the rural South, it also meant that I was a particular kind of white.

"I don't want to be a redneck," I'd sobbed between attempts at catching my breath. They were real tears—*no fueron lagrimas de cocodrilo.*

This was back in 1996. I was seven years old. My dad had just broken the news that we'd be moving to Tennessee, and all I could think about was how a change in physical location would change everything about who I was. I hadn't yet thought of how it might be tied to my linguistic inability.

Nowadays, I don't know if I'm more offended or relieved of being a *gringo*. In truth, I feel it's a little bit of both. But was being labeled *white* the reason why I identified as such? Or was it because I'd no better choice to on all those Scantron questionnaires? According to those little slips of paper, I had to be White, Not Latino. There was no way of identifying as both.

Ultimately, I think it's more to do with assimilation. I was born pasty—not cocoa beige (though later I'd be "brown" enough to be lumped together under the umbrella term *Mexican*). I glow bright red after too long in the sun, and I played baseball, first, before I ever scored a goal in soccer (even though later I'd be selected for the varsity football team as a place kicker before Coach figured out I wasn't really that Latino). And while Spanish might have been my first language spoken inside the home, nobody at school would've known it.

By the time I was in school, surrounded by white friends, I'd already made the unconscious choice to be one of Them. I'd learned to reason with a language that seemed traitorous to my ethnicity. In retrospect, it's probably the reason why when I felt so uncomfortable in my own skin.

Perhaps the same sentiment I experienced only months ago on the farm had been creeping silently behind me all these years. The feelings had taken root ever since the first time I'd heard that word—*gringo*. And like a vine whose cucumbers have been blanched by a lack of sun, I, too, had grown pale in comparison to what I thought I ought to be as a Latino.

I'd become as white as I'd labeled myself, or as white as I'd been labeled (I'm not entirely sure). Either way, being white is why my confidence shrinks to the size of a cucumber seed when in Latino company. It's because I know I can't fully express myself through ways in which they do. *Me rio (de Janeiro) cuando cuenten sus chistes*. I laugh, because I get the jokes (and colloquialisms, too) but ask me to do the same, to communicate effectively in a voice that's not my own, and I find myself silenced and up against a wall.

•••

Language does this to me. It creates borders where there might not otherwise be any. Its words distance me from those who I'm apparently most alike.

As a Latino or a *gringo*, I'm immersed in two separate worlds. I live in one where Spanish secretly conveys a subtle racism, along with distaste for food *que viene sin sazón*. I also live in a world where balding men with bulging bellies and crimson faces scream out, "English Motherfucker, this is America!" all while they line up at the local Mexican restaurant after church.

Words are why I've felt so far away from those who've been in closest proximity to me, but they're also the reason why I've been able to draw so near to some.

Despite how detached I'd felt from all my other relatives, home was most often a borderland: that "vague and undetermined place created by the emotional residue of an unnatural boundary." There, I was free to inhabit and explore the "psychic, social, and cultural terrains" of both my white peers and my browner ancestors without having to choose one over the other. This never caused any real problems with either my mom or my dad. Both my parents spoke fluently in either Spanish or English. And while I understood them perfectly when they'd speak the former tongue, I'd respond in what felt most natural—English—without ever feeling judged.

Though I didn't know it then, I'd encountered what cultural theorist Gloria Anzaldua called *la frontera* within the confines of my own home. For her, *fronteras* are the vague and undetermined places created by the emotional residue brought on by unnatural boundaries. For me, borderlands represented freedom and security.

I first experienced Anzaldua's writings in the Fall of 2016, (shortly after my experience on the farm) during graduate study at the University of Tennessee at Chattanooga. Anzaldua's theories of the marginal, the in-between, alongside her printed Spanglish encouraged me to entertain thoughts and ideas within the same, blended context. Everywhere I looked, borders became blurred. My thoughts became even more so, and I grew quiet. Calm.

It makes no sense to me, *ni lo puedo explicar con plastilina*, why I'd felt so offended by a word that, in retrospect, was likely said without the meaning I'd assigned it. It hadn't been a dangling modifier, it had precisely given rise to a separate identity. It had divided me up in two by its very meaning. Words, as Anzaldua stated, have the distinct capability to create divides between mankind. And one word, in particular, has been the reason why I divided my identity into being white and Latino, at one time or another, out of convenience—but never simultaneously as both.

Culturally, I'd been marked as a Latino since birth. By inheritance alone, I'd carry with me the ways of my people. But, I also belong to another population because I'm also not entirely Latino—not because of any cultural insecurity, but because I think in words that come from a whiter side of my brain. Linguistically, I'd been marked by the same whiteness I'd derived from the word *gringo*. The border it previously created within me only blinded me from my truth—that I am and I am not definable by a single word.

9   Sample Memoir

White Trash Soup
By Thomas Drake Farmer

"The springs become white trash soup during the summer," Victor explained in a raspy voice, as we drove down the unpaved, sandy roads near his house in O'Brien, Florida. Victor, who is in his mid-thirties and is tall, slim, and handsome was referencing a freshwater spring called Royal, one of many that line the edges of Suwannee River. It was a hot, humid Memorial Day in north-central Florida. I was riding in the back of my friend Will's red Toyota SUV. Will is Victor's younger brother. I guessed that was Victor's way of telling that the springs would be crowded that day. But it sounded more like a warning, like the sentiment that resonated below the surface of Victor's statement was telling us to watch out.

That summer was the first time I'd visited O'Brien. My girlfriend and I had driven down to Jacksonville for a few days to visit a friend of mine from college, Will. While we were there, the three of us—plus two more friends—decided to take a day and a half trip, driving two hours west to Will's hometown for a chance to swim in the freshwater springs. Pulling into town, William launched into a spiel par for the course for someone showing their friends around the place they'd grown up. We learned that O'Brien is an unincorporated community and has only one paved road, on which can be found the town's only stoplight. We learned that the town's only corner store is adjacent to the only stoplight in O'Brien; that single block was the town's big city center. Next came the snapshot history lesson: back fifty years or so ago, O'Brien was notorious for its destination as a hideaway from the law. When in trouble, convicts would make a dash for O'Brien and, eventually, they would make their home in the woods and along the Suwannee. We were told that, as an homage to the influx of those running from the law, one of the local springs was named Convict, and that this seemed to set the "mood" for the area. Now, the town is largely agricultural—potatoes, not the typical Florida oranges like we might think. Will paused on this last bit of information, as if waiting to hit us with a big, stereotype defying reveal. He also told us that working on a potato farm was the worst job he'd ever had, and that he can't believe how hard those who labor on the farm year-round work.

•••

Of course, *white trash* was a phrase I'd heard—and admittedly, used—before as a joke, an insult, or a genuine question. I grew up in Southeast Tennessee, and had family in Alabama and Georgia. The house that I grew up in, on Signal Mountain, was in a neighborhood with paved roads and a cul-de-sac, but I often found myself having to clarify its exact whereabouts with some version of the following phrase: "well, it's actually on the backside of the mountain. Towards Soddy-Daisy and Dunlap." This admission—though not embarrassing to me—more often than not garnered a reaction from anyone who lived on the front (read: wealthier side) of the mountain.

When I was younger—ten or eleven, I can't remember precisely—I went on a road trip with my parents and grandparents, my aunt and uncle, and three of my cousins. We took nearly an entire summer and drove from Chattanooga, to Alaska, and back. My parents, grandparents, and I piled into one truck and towed a pull-behind camper. My aunt, uncle, and cousins piled into a truck with a truck bed camper nested on its back. I don't remember where we were, exactly, but at one point on the trip my youngest cousin, who was barely five at the time, saw a similar camper, pointed to it, and, in clunky kid-speech, called it *white trash*. My family laughed and explained that just because this person had a camper on the back of their truck, didn't mean they were white trash. Also, my aunt and uncle asked if *they* were white trash since they had a similar camper. But how do you dive into those nuances with a five-year-old?

•••

Will's family—his parents, grandparents, Victor, and Victor's wife and children—all live on the same stretch of land bordering the Suwannee River, about a half-mile off the nearest road. Their driveway is a double-track path underneath oaks and maples. We arrived in the early evening and were greeted by Will's parents. The house, a modular home on stilts (as is customary in Florida, due to frequent flooding) was nestled among a cluster of trees. A barn sits adjacent. As we sat on the front porch and talked with Will's dad, who is a short man with leathery hands, an iron grip, and clear, bluish gray eyes, Will explains to me that his dad has a fickle relationship with some of the nearby farm owners, where he often picks up work fixing their machinery. Apparently the problem, for the farmers, isn't that Victor does poor work, but that he gets too close with migrant workers, of which there are many in O'Brien.

The next morning, we loaded up the car and set out for spring-hopping. We drove down the long, sandy double track driveway and turned left, out onto the town's single paved road. That's when Victor made the comment about white trash soup.

When I heard Victor refer to the crowds of people swimming in the freshwater spring as white trash, and when I paused to think about the implications of the spring water as a soup, I chuckled. To say I didn't, and instead took some supposed moral ground wherein I launched into a diatribe about the historical implications of a racialized and stigmatized term like white trash, would be false. For one thing, I didn't yet have the language to back up such statements, even if I wanted to. More so, the truth is that I found Victor's metaphor, and the image it conjured, funny.

But it also made me slightly uncomfortable, not least because I was a visitor to the area. What right, I wondered, did I have to come to a rural town in central Florida and laugh at the phrase *white trash soup*? And where did Victor fall into this equation? I didn't view *him* as white trash, after all. But Victory, like many others in O'Brien, was living in a stilted modular home; he had long-abandoned project cars and minibikes strewn across his front lawn. Next to his house sat a Winnebago, which Victor had added a porch to and turned into his own private space. So, what delineated him from those about whom he was speaking? And further—what, if anything, separated me from white trash? As we drove along, I tried to be fair; I didn't know these people, or their situations. I watched the two-story mobile homes and front lawns sprinkled with broken down cars, tractors, and motorcycles drift by and I couldn't come up with an alternative term for what I was seeing. On that trip to the springs in Florida, whiteness became visible to me in a way I hadn't previously considered.

...

Here's something that makes the conversation of white trash a bit more difficult for me: I have family who fit the white trash stereotype. There's a rift that runs through my family dynamic that is largely—secretly,

I think—centered around a notion of white trash. Members of my family are consistently in-between jobs, strung out, or in jail, and make no real effort to change their situation. I also have family members who are affluent, with generally accepted "good jobs"—engineers, upper management, etc.—and who pride themselves on their social standing. For one thing, this stark difference is noticeable. It has also caused tensions where certain family members refuse to attend the holiday parties of others, as they feel unwelcome or judged due to their class status. I've family members who—quite literally—live in a "mansion on the hill," and family who have lived for months in an extended stay hotel near I-75.

Admittedly, this messy issue is further complicated by the fact that I don't want to align myself with white trash, but I also don't want to align myself with the upper-class, affluent types. I take a strange sort of pride in my liminal position, even if it's a constructed position. That I can choose how I want to align myself and be successful, more or less, in doing so is problematic.

Because of this, the older I get, the more I became embarrassed of my own situation: I went to a private high-school, a good college (many of my cousins never went), and now, as a graduate student studying the very system of which they are a part. In other words, I can float between the two sides of my family almost seamlessly, adjusting my language and mannerisms according to my situation. And, in fact, I do exactly that. I code switch. At family gatherings, I find that my diction shifts. Depending on who I'm talking to, my vocabulary also inadvertently shifts, and my vowels get slightly elongated. I also make attempts to talk about subjects, like hunting and sports, that I would otherwise never discuss. I've thought about it, but I still can't come up with exactly how I feel about this. Does my awareness of being able to shift between discourse communities make me a bad person? Or is it okay that I do it as long as I'm aware of what's going on.

In Florida, I saw the same in Will; his mannerisms relaxed and his diction shifted.

•••

We pulled into the parking lot at the Royal and, just as Victor had suggested, it was crowded. I couldn't shake the metaphor of the soup. Walking to the spring I saw lifted trucks with chipped paint, confederate flag bikini tops a few sizes too small, and cheap beer as far as the eye could see. I saw women, pregnant and with cigarettes dangling from their lips, warning nearby children to "cut it out." From the water, "toss me another" echoed like a mantra.

We took a dip in Royal, but eventually found it too crowded and opted, instead, to drive to the various springs until we found one that was less hectic. Or, that was the reason we agreed upon in the car. Perhaps we simply found it too "trashy."

•••

Aside from the swarms of people, something else caught my attention at the spring. I noticed that the majority—if not all, it's difficult to remember—of the families at the springs were white, which was curious given Will and his dad had both told me about the large number of migrant workers in O'Brien.

"Do the migrant workers and families not come to the springs often?" I asked.

Will explained that the working and under-class whites don't get along with the migrant workers, despite being in nearly the same economic position. He said that is a large reason why his dad wasn't liked by many of the farmers and white farm workers. He associated with the migrant workers, and this caused tension.

"Yeah," he's told me in the past. "Dad takes lunch with the migrant workers, brings them over to the house for dinner, teaches them how to work on their cars—if they have them—or fix the farm equipment. And that doesn't go over too well with some of them farmers—not all of them feel that way, but some."

Will also told me that it's nearly impossible to navigate the local grocery store on a Friday afternoon, as there's always a massive line of workers trying to wire money back home to their families.

"It's best to just not go on Friday. It gets incredibly crowded," he said.

•••

The next day, we packed the car and headed back to Jacksonville, leaving Victor and Will's parents and thanking them for their hospitality. We passed the barn Will's dad had built, with all of its tools, trinkets, and projects; we passed Victor's house, where the Winnebago and vintage cars sat, fixed, in the grass. I think I'd largely put Victor's comment out of mind, but his nonchalance in using the term white trash soup stuck with me. More puzzling was the fact that I have, on other occasions, heard him say that he's "one step away"—or some version of that—from being white trash himself. I've never gotten much clarification from him on what it is that keeps him from actually being white trash.

•••

A few years after that trip to O'Brien, and I have some language to put to my thoughts. Because of social theorists like Matt Wray, I can respond, when questioned or pausing to reflect, that "white trash...is racialized and classed...'good to think with' when it comes to issues of race and class in the U.S. because the term foregrounds whiteness and working-class and underclass poverty..." (*Introduction* 4). I know now that the phrase, itself, serves as a boundary term that delineates and marginalizes poor, rural whites based on class and, consequentially, race. I now understand the history of the term a little bit better, grasping more fully how the term has been used for centuries as to other poor rural whites. I realize now that perhaps my own discomfort with the term—or how to view those I see under its stigmatized shroud—is only playing into a long-standing tradition of attempting to reconcile why some whites aren't "quite white," to borrow from the title to one of Wray's books. In other words, I'm trying to see the ways in which these groups are seen as not white, to see what qualifications are needed to be "white," and to hopefully intentionally work against them.

•••

Now, as I'm writing this essay, I'm thinking back to the various times the term white trash has slipped past me, unnoticed and without a second thought. I'm replaying scenes of driving past mobile homes and small houses with faded cedar siding and patched tin roofs; I'm recalling when my cousins and I would race ATVs through the woods that surrounded my house and play, barefoot, in the mud on rainy days. I'm thinking of road trip to Alaska and hearing my cousin, at the time barely five years old, point to a camper on the back of a single cab truck, saying "Look, Mama—white trash."

10   Sample Critical Dialogue

**Facebook Status Transcript: Imagined Critical Dialogue
of Whiteness as a Racialized Space**
Constructed by Faith Jones

The transcript you are viewing is one I imagined taking place on my Facebook status today. We were all engaged in a discussion of racial rhetorics started by my initial question of Obama's use of racial rhetoric in "A More Perfect Union" speech from 2008. I am a University of Tennessee at Chattanooga graduate studying rhetoric, and I was thankful to have Kristi McDuffie, Ersula Ore, Brent Staples, and Patrick Lukens comment. Each of these individuals are scholars of racial rhetorics in their own careers. We were able to discuss the idea of whiteness as a racialized space. I was inspired after reading Ore's essay about this exact topic and would be honored to have such a strong response.

I wished to write out the transcript to give more background into who was engaging in the comment section. I'll be following in the order of comments. First, Kristi McDuffie is the Interim Director of Rhetoric at the University of Illinois. Her interests range from digital writing to race and whiteness rhetorics. Second, Ersula Ore is the Lincoln Professor of Ethics in The School of Social Transformation and Assistant Professor of African & African American Studies and Rhetoric at Arizona State University. She evaluates aggrieved communities within a post-emancipation historical context. Third, Brent Staples received his Ph.D. in psychology from the University of Chicago and has sat on *The New York Times* editorial board since 1990. Finally, Patrick Lukens has served as a policy analyst for the Arizona Board of Regents and currently an independent scholar, and a faculty member, in the Arizona community college system. You may also find screenshots of the Facebook conversation attached to this transcript.

• • •

Faith Jones: Today's #RhetQuest I'm taking a look at former-President Obama's "A More Perfect Union Speech" and his discussion of race. At the time, Obama was the U.S. senator from Illinois running for the Democratic Party nomination for presidency in 2007–2008. Many cite this as his address on race but how effective was it overall from a national perspective? As a rhetor himself, he's having to utilize racial rhetorics in order to appeal to white voters.

Kristi McDuffie: [This is a great #RhetQuest. Here's just a quick background of how those events unfolded:] His "A More Perfect Union" speech in 2008 [was] given to diffuse public outrage about comments made by Obama's pastor, Reverend Jeremiah Wright (72). *Good Morning America* released several excerpts from 2001 to 2003 sermons from his pastor [...] The media and public were outraged at remarks that they perceived to be inflammatory, racist, anti-Christian, and anti-American (73).

Faith Jones: Despite distancing himself from the media storm, the speech he gave would be a turning point for his future nomination and his presidency.

Kristi McDuffie: [Right.] Although [he] was the first black President of the United States, he is considerably mum on issues of race. Obama's racial rhetorics during his two presidential terms shows that avoiding racial topics is necessary for him to stay in favor with white voters (71–73).

Faith Jones: I think you're onto some good criticism here. But first, let's break down what racial rhetorics means. How would you classify Obama's racial rhetorics during his "A More Perfect Union" speech?

Kristi McDuffie: I find that [it's] because of Obama's appeals to whiteness within the speech that made it so effective for mainstream audiences (74).

Faith Jones: "Appealing to whiteness" and "effectiveness for mainstream audiences" suggests there are two abstract spaces working against each other. It'd be one space considered the norm, and the other would be, well, "other"—everything (and everyone) that's considered outside of the norm.

Ersula Ore: Space gains its racialized character through a mix of racial-spatial practices: legal, social, economic, and political practices that designate particular spaces as exclusively inhabitable by particular raced bodies [...] Non-white bodies were [...] symbols of lack while white bodies stood as the representative norm (260). Oftentimes the most strategic option for rhetors that lack the privilege of being the somatic norm is to find creative ways of mitigating white imaginings of "the dangerous trespasser" while maintaining a personal sense of self-respect (259).

Brent Staples: [This reminds me of a personal story that may help contextualize your point.] After dark, on the warrenlike streets of Brooklyn where I live, I often see women who fear the worst from me. They seem to have set their faces on neutral, and with their purse straps strung across their chests bandolier-style, they forge ahead as though bracing themselves against being tackled ("Just").

Faith Jones: In this case, Brent, you were navigating a space where you "appeared" threatening which ultimately points to the lack of privilege you had in that space.

Brent Staples: [Yes.] The most frightening of these confusions occurred in the late 1970s and early 1980s, when I worked as a journalist in Chicago. One day, rushing into the office of a magazine I was writing for with a deadline story in hand, I was mistaken for a burglar. The office manager called security and, with an ad hoc posse, pursued me through the labyrinthine halls, nearly to my editor's door. I had no way of proving who I was. I could only move briskly toward the company of someone who knew me ("Just").

Faith Jones: Wow, so quite literally an example of "the dangerous trespasser." You're navigating these historically white spaces where someone like me, a white woman, could navigate with my privilege, and as a result, you're seen as the outsider or "other" who lacks the privilege I have—which is just outright racial injustice.

Brent Staples: Over the years, I learned to smother the rage I felt at so often being taken for a criminal. Not to do so would surely have led to madness. I now take precautions to make myself less threatening [...] I employ what has proved to be an excellent tension-reducing measure: I whistle melodies from Beethoven and Vivaldi and the more popular classical composers [...] Virtually everybody seems to sense that a mugger wouldn't be warbling bright, sunny selections from Vivaldi's Four Seasons. It is my equivalent of the cowbell that hikers wear when they know they are in bear country ("Just").

Ersula Ore: [Thank you, Brent. That's exactly my point. His own experience is how] I see Obama's rendition of "whistling Vivaldi"[;] as a response [or creative way] to the rhetorical burden of being a non-white body in white racialized space [...] That is, [racial] spatial awareness is a rhetorical necessity for non-white rhetors operating in white space (260).

Faith Jones: The traditionally white rhetorical history of the White House highlights why a nonwhite rhetor may need to 1) recognize whiteness as a racialized space, and 2) "whistle Vivaldi" in order to signal commonality to a white nation.

Kristi McDuffie: Despite race and whiteness studies work highlighting Obama's color-blind race rhetorics in the writings of Eduardo Bonilla-Silva, David Frank and Mark Lawrence McPhail, and Tim Wise, rhetorical studies have not significantly integrated these critiques into their investigations of Obama's race rhetorics, perhaps because, as I argue in this chapter, rhetoric scholars have come to equate any direct confrontation with race as evidence of progress on race relations in the United States, even though I find that the speech appeals to white privilege through color-blind rhetorical strategies (72).

Kristi McDuffie: [However,] rhetoricians and other interested parties studying Obama's racial rhetorics, from journalists to pundits to everyday citizens, should consider the effects of neoliberalism and color-blind racial rhetorics in speeches such as these in order to avoid participating in the maintenance of white supremacy and white privilege (73).

Ersula Ore: [Yes,] I see little difference [...] between twenty-first century practices [...] that enthymemically racialize space and mid-twentieth century signs of legalized segregation that read "No Blacks Allowed." If we acknowledge, rather than ignore, America's legacy of racism, segregation, and racialized violence, then it becomes difficult to read Obama effigies [...] as anything other than twenty-first century iterations of a tradition of rhetorically racializing certain spaces as spaces for "White Only" (258).

Faith Jones: Whiteness operates as invisible yet front and center—especially considering positions of typical white power. When whiteness faces a "foreign challenger," it has warranted unprecedented racism. *Patrick Lukens* offers great examples of unprecedented racism toward Mexican immigrants/Mexican Americans— —the *Andrade* federal ruling in 1935. U.S. federal judge John Knight ruled to deny three Mexican immigrants (one named Timoteo Andrade) petitions for naturalization in 1935. It was in this case Knight handed down a firm legal definition making Mexican nationals ineligible for U.S. naturalization in an era with unclear parameters surrounding Mexican racial status.

Patrick Lukens: [Thanks for the mention!] Within the same general time frame as Judge Knight's ruling, and because of the political realities of the era, Mexican American civil rights activists had been pushing their own agenda of having themselves racially classified as white. Therefore, asserting whiteness became a common approach to acquiring U.S. citizenship in the early twentieth century (8).

Ersula Ore: [Here lies another example] of philosophical concepts made material through legal doctrine: The U.S. Constitution, federal and state laws, and landmark decisions like *Dred Scott v. Sandford* (1857)[,] *Plessy v. Ferguson* (1896)[, and Knight's federal ruling] (260).

Patrick Lukens: [Yes, and I'd also add the Fourteenth Amendment (i.e., "equal protection").] An ideology called eugenics played a role in the scientific thinking behind racial definitions of the era. In Europe and North America, the eugenicists used the science of the time to demonstrate the supposed superiority of the Anglo-Saxon race. It was also within that policy context that Mexican American civil rights activists had to operate. Some issues that Mexican Americans faced were that most white Americans associated them with Mexican immigrants, used *Mexican* to indicate a racial rather than a national identity, and, in some parts of the United States, implemented segregation against Mexican Americans just as they segregated black Americans. So to many Mexican American activists, obtaining civil rights also meant being racially classified as white (16).

Faith Jones: Right. It dismisses people of color who are outside the black/white binary.

Patrick Lukens: The primary issue at hand here is what scholars have termed the "black/white binary paradigm." [It has placed racial identity into two, categorical binaries of black and white.] The paradigm oversimplifies racial ideas in much the same way that a freshman-level survey history course takes a broad view of centuries of time (9)

Faith Jones: Great point, Patrick. Setting our sights for the future, how should we continue approaching racial rhetorics? I find that now, more than ever, racial rhetorics have become a pivotal study within the current presidential administration—statements and policy that are actively promoting the silence of minorities and reinforcing white racialized spaces.

Kristi McDuffie: [...] I advocate that we can celebrate the United States, electing a black President while still problematizing the race and whiteness rhetorics influencing and emerging from a political and social system placing such successes neatly within white racial ideologies. Examining those color-blind rhetorical positions means opening possibilities for redressing whiteness and its stronghold in our social and political landscape. In this way, rhetorical studies can engage in racial justice rather than remaining complicit in existing race relations (83).

Faith Jones: Looking at pieces of rhetoric, like "A More Perfect Union," and recognizing how people of color must navigate color-blind rhetoric in order to appeal to their audiences. Only this time we should be calling for racial justice. Actions speaking louder than words.

Ersula Ore: [I agree with you Kristi, I believe it is still important to analyze current racial relations [...] The pursuit of such rhetorical performances is to render one's-self more *familiar* than *strange* (262) [...]

Faith Jones: I see you drawing from Kenneth Burke here. In a rhetorical situation like "A More Perfect Union," Obama is operating as the performer to his audience. It's his goal to be able to act out tropes of whiteness in order to be more familiar than strange in his performance to become the President of the United States.

Ersula Ore: [Yes.] Obama's whistling is not a form of "passing for white." Rather, it reflects an available means of contending with the racialized rhetorical constraints of whiteness (268).

Faith Jones: This has been such a great discussion! Seriously, thanks you all.

Works Cited

Lukens, Patrick D. A Quiet Victory for Latino Rights: FDR and the Controversy Over Whiteness. University of Arizona Press, 2012.

McDuffie, Kristi. "Color-Blind Rhetoric In Obama's 2008 'Race Speech': The Appeal To Whiteness And The Disciplining Of Racial Rhetorical Studies." *Rhetorics of Whiteness: Postracial Hauntings In Popular Culture, Social Media, And Education*, edited by Tammie M Kennedy et al., Southern Illinois University Press, 2017, pp. 71–85.

Ore, Ersula. "Whiteness As Racialized Space: Obama And The Rhetorical Constraints Of Phenotypical Blackness." *Rhetorics of Whiteness: Postracial Hauntings In Popular Culture, Social Media, And Education*, edited by Tammie M Kennedy et al., Southern Illinois University Press, 2017, pp. 256–270.

Staples, Brent. "Just Walk On By." *Scribd*, www.scribd.com/doc/37177242/Just-Walk-on-by-Brent-Staples

11   Second Sample Critical Dialogue

What Will Future Generations Look Like?
An Imagined Online Critical Dialogue about White Normalcy and Black Identity in Pop Culture

Christine Smalley has entered the chat

@csmalls7 is typing...

Christine Smalley   10/23/19
@csmalls7   1:17 PM

Hi!

While everyone is getting logged on, I just want to take the time to say thank you for those both reading and participating in this live chat. My name is Christine Smalley, and I am a student at the University of Tennessee at Chattanooga studying the rhetorics of whiteness. After broaching many topics this semester, my goal here is to talk specifically about how white normalcy and black erasure play out in pop culture. This topic covers a wide range of issues and will hopefully make for a riveting discussion and debate. Considering that pop culture is aimed mainly at younger generations and directly impacts how the future could play out, I think it is important to point out what racial dynamics are being presented in popular culture.

To expand on these concerns, I have asked a few specific speakers to join me in this chat today, including Toni Morrison, bell hooks, Tim Wise, and Anita DeRouen. Toni Morrison is the author of *Playing in the Dark: Whiteness and the Literary Imagination*, a three-part literary criticism of well-known American literature and the Africanist presence within them. bell hooks is an American author, professor, and social activist with a focus on intersectionality of race and systems of oppression. Tim Wise is an American writer and anti-racist activist. Finally, Anita DeRouen is the director of writing and teaching at Millsaps College where she focuses on media culture and its representation of racial identity.

@bellhooks has entered the chat

@TimWise has entered the chat

@csmalls7 is typing...

Christine Smalley   10/23/19
@csmalls7   1:24 PM

My first question to get this chat going, then, will be directed at Tim Wise. *@TimWise*, Christmas time is fast approaching, so I feel it is relevant to bring up the issue regarding Santa Claus and how this figure is presented to children all over the world through the use of art and other forms of pop culture. You spoke on this subject not too long ago concerning the claim from Megyn Kelly that Santa Claus is white, he just is, and there can be no question about it. Obviously, this poses a problem when it comes to young generations of children who still believe in this figure.

What are your thoughts about how this assumption that Santa Claus is white is still in place?

@ToniMorrison has entered the chat

@AnitaDeRouen has entered the chat

@TimWise is typing...

Tim Wise   10/23/19
@TimWise   1:35 PM

[Let me just set the scene by taking you back to an instance of Christmas shopping I found myself in.] I too [had] been making the pilgrimage to shopping centers, both to purchase desired items, and also to observe others in the process of this sociologically fascinating ritual. As someone who regularly writes about racism, you can probably imagine that I have long been intrigued by the way in which holiday symbolism replicates the notions of whiteness as rightness, and acts to reinforce, however subtly, racial supremacy. It was then that I found myself at the mall, passing a line of parents and their children, waiting to have a few seconds alone with Santa. You know Santa, right? The big white guy who only works one day a year and yet no one calls him lazy; the big white guy who exploits elfin labor in a sweatshop for no pay while his wife does all the housework, and yet no one calls him a slave master; the big white guy who invades millions of homes on Christmas Eve, and yet no one arrests him for breaking and entering. Though one can see a few Santas of color in malls around the country lately, I think we can all agree this is pretty absurd. After all, if Santa were black, there's little question he'd have been shot dead years ago in the vestibule of some New York City apartment by the NYPD's Street Crimes Unit. Really now, how could the cop be sure that toy gun he was bringing to the kid inside wasn't real? Better safe than sorry, and anyway, that bright red suit would make him a logical target, seeing as how red is the color favored by members of the Bloods street gang (Wise "Dreaming").

But it wasn't this kind of irony about a black Santa that animated the comment I heard while strolling through the mall that day. No, it was pure racial resentment and nothing else leading the white woman, child in tow, to say to her friend, "Don't you think it's silly to have these Black Santas? Everybody's trying to be so P.C. I mean, come on, a Black Santa? Everyone knows Santa is white." Her friend agreed. Everyone knows Santa (a make believe entity for those who haven't figured it out yet) is white (Wise "Dreaming").

@csmalls7 is typing...

Christine Smalley   10/23/19
@csmalls7   1:40 PM

I agree with you that this seems to be an issue that is staying prevalent because of parents' refusal to entertain any other option about it. Why do you think this is? Is this something learned by the older generations through something else?

@TimWise is typing...

Tim Wise   10/23/19
@TimWise   1:47 PM

[Your comment and question bring me to my next point.] It all made sense [...] once I passed the woman and noticed the holiday cards in her bag. The ones with the calming, soothing face of Jesus staring back at me. You know the Jesus I'm talking about right? The one with the pale skin, blue eyes, and rock-star good looks? Yeah, that one: the one envisioned by pretty much every one of European descent (and several of non-European descent for that matter) for the last five hundred years. So long as our culture pictures Adam, Eve, Moses, Jesus, Mary, the Apostles, and even God "himself" as fair-skinned, despite the obvious preposterousness of such representations, we will continue to plant the seeds of racial supremacy in the hearts and minds of millions. [including the very generation that pop culture is directed at] After all, to believe that divinity is white like you leads one to easily assume that others are somehow less complete, less than human If God supposedly made man in his image, and God is always portrayed as a bearded white guy (kinda like Santa without the suit), how big a leap is it — especially for children whose introduction to religion is always nine-tenths forced propaganda anyway — to assume that persons of color are somehow not full and equal "children of God?" Not to mention the sexist aspect of the male sky-God imagery, of course, which is a whole different can of worms (Wise "Dreaming").

@csmalls is typing...

Christine Smalley   10/23/19
@csmalls7   1:52 PM

Ah, yes, the old Warner Sallman image. Thanks for reminding us of that, Mr. Wise. That image of a white Jesus is definitely something older generations have grown up with and found normalized, which is now being projected onto the children. Children are easily influenced, especially when it comes to things they see their parents and others they respect and look up to doing.

@AniteDeRouen is typing...

Anita DeRouen   10/23/19
@AnitaDeRouen   2:01 PM

[Tim Wise is correct in the erasure of blackness in religious iconography and holiday images, which steers this conversation in the direction of black erasure in popular media—namely in] television dramas featuring women of color in leading or narratively central roles. [We can] limit our focus to the shows *Suits* and *Scandal* [...] the stories of two black female attorneys at the helm of powerful institutions who must frequently use their power to protect whiteness from itself and others. [The two leads are essentially erased from their own narratives]: Olivia Pope still becomes marginalized in the service of whiteness in her own story, much in the same way Jessica Pearson lacks centrality in the narrative that centers on the law firm she owns and runs (DeRouen 54–56).

@csmalls7 is typing...

Christine Smalley   10/23/19
@csmalls7   2:08 PM

This is a good topic to broach, Ms. DeRouen. TV series are a big part of pop culture nowadays and a lot of young folks are looking to them and to movies to see themselves represented on the big screen. How do you think these two characters work to further establish white normativity?

@AnitaDeRouen is typing...

Anita DeRouen   10/23/19
@AnitaDeRouen   2:17 PM

The characters we examine serve the interests of white men as well as further deployment of systematic whiteness instead of challenging or revealing the power and privilege whiteness confers. [This] exploration reveals how these characters pay what **@bellhooks** calls the "price" for "assimilation into the dominant culture" by their "collusion in supporting the thinking and practice of white supremacy. Whether in their personal or professional lives, Jessica and Olivia operate from a sphere of whiteness, their racial identities textually invisible [...] [and other] WOC characters rarely speak from their racial identity position [...] even those characters who do speak from the margins continue to advance whiteness agendas (DeRouen 55–59).

@bellhooks is typing...

bell hooks   10/23/19
@bellhooks   2:26 PM

[Thanks for the mention, Ms. DeRouen. The entertainment industry plays a big part in race dynamics, not only erasing black female identity, but allowing white females to profit from the theft of black culture identity. This is seen in how] white women "stars" like Madonna, Sandra Bernhard, and many others publicly name their interests in, and appropriation of, black culture as yet another sign of their radical chic. To white and other nonblack consumers, this gives them a special flavor, an added spice. After all it is a very recent historical phenomenon for any white girl to be able to get some mileage out of flaunting her fascination and envy of blackness. The thing about envy is that it is always ready to destroy, erase, take-over, and consume the desired object. That's exactly what Madonna attempts to do when she appropriates and commodifies aspects of black culture. Needless to say this kind of fascination is a threat. It endangers. (hooks 307).

@csmalls7 is typing...

Christine Smalley   10/23/19
@csmalls7   2:38 PM

I agree with you, Ms. hooks, that cultural appropriation practically screams erasure and uncaring on the white person's part when it comes to the injustice the culture they are appropriating endures. Would you all say there's a difference between someone like Madonna trying to appropriate black culture and someone who is white claiming to actually be black? **@TimWise**, some thoughts on this? You address this issue of mimicry in your essay about Rachel Dolezal. How is this different from what Ms. hooks has to say about Madonna?

@TimWise is typing...

Tim Wise   10/23/19
@TimWise   2:51 PM

[As Ms. hooks notes, cultural appropriation poses a threat to the race that can't get away with the things that a white person mimicking can.] In a country where being black increases your likelihood of being unemployed, poor, rejected for a bank loan, suspected of wrongdoing and profiled as a criminal, being arrested or even shot by police, the mind boggles at the decision of Rachel Dolezal some years ago to begin posing as an African American woman. Indeed, it has real implications for white people seeking to work in solidarity with people of color, whether in the BlackLivesMatter movement, Moral Mondays in North Carolina, or any other component of the modern civil rights and antiracism struggle (Wise "Mimicry").

@bellhooks is typing...

bell hooks   10/23/19
@bellhooks   3:04 PM

[Along with what you say about Dolezal believing working in solidarity is a way to justify cultural appropriation, Mr. Wise] I [once] read an interview with Madonna where she talked about her envy of black culture, where she stated that she wanted to be black as a child. It is a sign of what privilege to be able to "see" blackness and black culture from a standpoint where only rich culture of opposition black people have created in resistance marks and defines us. Such a perspective enables one to ignore white supremacist domination and the hurt it inflicts *via* oppression, exploitation, and everyday wounds and pains. White folks who do not see black pain never really understand the complexity of black pleasure. And it is no wonder then that when they attempt to imitate the joy in living which they see as the "essence" of soul and blackness, their cultural productions may have an air of sham and falseness that may titillate and even move white audiences yet leave many black folks cold (hooks 308).

@ToniMorrison is typing...

Toni Morrison   10/23/19
@ToniMorrison
3:13 PM

[It may be a new thing for white folks to want to assimilate into black culture, Ms. hooks and Mr. Wise, but black erasure is an old concept that dates back to the earliest form of pop culture: American literature. This acted to further the hierarchy that places white men at the top, just as Ms. DeRouen points out.] For some time now I have been thinking about the validity or vulnerability of a certain set of assumptions conventionally accepted among literary historians and critics and circulate as "knowledge." This knowledge holds that traditional, canonical American literature is free of, uninformed, and unshaped by the four-hundred-year-old presence of, first, Africans and then African-Americans in the United States. It assumes that this presence—which shaped the body politic, the constitution, and the entire history of the culture—has had no significant place or consequence in the origin and development of that culture's literature. [This aspect is seen] in the works of Edgar Allan Poe, [...] Will Cather, [...], Ernest Hemingway, [...] Flannery O'Connor, [...] [and] Faulkner. [All of which are read by students in literature courses] (Morrison 4–14).

@csmalls7 is typing...

Christine Smalley   10/23/19
@csmalls7   3:27 PM

As a student currently, I must agree that a good portion of my education has focused on reading literature by and about white men with people of color represented as on the margins or as stock figures. These are all great points and takes, which have expanded my thinking on the subject of racial issues in canonical texts, as well as in pop culture. I had never taken in to account how far spread such racial stereotyping and erasure were—from Santa Claus to popular series to the authors I'm currently reading in American literature. You've all given me a lot to think about and study up on.

My last question is this: what can we do as a society to combat these issues?

@AnitaDeRouen is typing...

Anita DeRouen   10/23/19
@AnitaDeRouen   3:33 PM

[As far as black erasure in media], what we discover in the end is that it is not enough to engage in mere representation of WOC in mainstream narratives; instead, social transformation can only come about if we, the audience, are provided both the knowledge of and the tools to dismantle white hegemony (DeRouen 68).

@bellhooks is typing...

bell hooks   10/23/19
@bellhooks   3:41 PM

[In regards to Madonna and producers of shows like *Scandal* who hope to profit from black culture], I can only say that this doesn't sound like liberation to me. Perhaps when Madonna explores those memories of her white working-class childhood in a troubled family in a way that enables her to understand intimately the politics of exploration, domination, and submission, she will have a deeper connection with oppositional black culture (hooks 315–316).

@ToniMorrison is typing...

Toni Morrison   10/23/19
@ToniMorrison   3:47 PM

[Even with traditional literary study, a way to do some of the dismantling we've been getting at would be to critically interrogate the] ways in which a nonwhite, Africanist presence and personae have been constructed—invented—in the United States, and of the literary uses this fabricated presence has served. [...] All of us, readers and writers, are bereft when criticism remains too polite or too fearful to notice a disrupting darkness before its eyes (Morrison 90–91).

@TimWise is typing...

Tim Wise   10/23/19
@TimWise   3:58 PM

There is a lesson here for us, for we who are white and care deeply about racial equity, justice and liberation, and the lesson is this: authentic anti-racist white identity is what we must cultivate. We cannot shed our skin, nor our privileges like an outdated overcoat. They are not accessories to be donned or not as one pleases, but rather, persistent reminders of the society that is not yet real, which is why we must work with people of color to overturn the system that bestows those privileges. But the key word here is *with* people of color, not *as* them. We must be willing to do the difficult work of finding a different way to live in *this* skin (Wise "Mimicry").

@csmalls7 is typing...

Christine Smalley   10/23/19
@csmalls7   4:05 PM

Thank you all so much for participating in this chat today and for providing such thoughtful insight into an ongoing issue. As critical whiteness scholars, your work is important for giving students like me the tools for critically engaging with culture, as opposed to being a passive object of it. Likewise, your work gives producers of cultural artifacts important considerations for considering—and hopefully avoiding—harmful appropriations or erasure of the culture of non-dominant groups.

This chat has been closed for comments.

Works Cited

DeRouen, Anita. "Must(n't) See TV: Hidden Whiteness in Representations of Women of Color." *Rhetorics of Whiteness Postracial Hauntings in Popular Cultur, Social Media, and Education.* ed. By Tammie M. Kennedy et al., Southern Illinois University Press, 2017, pp. 54–70.

hooks, bell. "Madonna: Plantation Mistress or Soul Sister." *Black on White: Black Writers on What it Means to Be White*. Ed. David R. Roediger. Schocken Books, 1998. pp. 38–53.

Morrison, Toni. *Playing in the Dark: Whiteness and the Literary Imagination*. Harvard University Press, 1992, pp. 4–91.

Wise, Tim. "Dreaming of a Non-White Christmas: Santa, Jesus and the Symbolism of Racial Supremacy." timwise.org, http://www.timwise.org/2000/12/dreaming-of-a-non-white-christmas-santa-jesus-and-the-symbolism-of-racial-supremacy/, accessed October 2019.

Wise, Tim. "Mimicry is not Solidarity: Of Allies, Rachel Dolezal and the Creation of Antiracist White Identity." timwise.org, http://www.timwise.org/2015/06/mimicry-is-not-solidarity-of-allies-rachel-dolezal-and-the-creation-of-antiracist-white-identity/, accessed October 2019.

We wish to recognize and mourn the loss of such an important scholar-writer as Toni Morrison, yet honor her words in this imagined dialogue because they continue to live and speak with and to us.

12 Cultural Studies Rhetorical Analysis Assignment

Genre: Cultural Studies Rhetorical Analysis
Audience: Academic Audience; imagine your essay would be included in an edited collection for undergraduates studying whiteness
Length: 5.5–7 pp. (10–15 for grads), double-spaced, typed in 10–12 pt font in MLA format
Peer Review: bring 3 full-draft copies
Essay due:

12.1 *Assignment*

For this assignment, you will select a *single popular/media* (magazine, video, t.v. program or movie, speech, catalog, advertisement, etc.) *representation of whiteness* to analyze from a cultural studies rhetorical perspective: analyzing production, circulation, and reception, as well as other relevant rhetorical appeals. Your purpose is to help your audience consider how the artifact functions rhetorically at a particular moment in American (or other) culture. Doing so, your analysis should help us better understand how race functions as a rhetorical and social construct and, possibly, help us think in ways that are more ethical with respect to race and race relations. For kairos, it is best to select an artifact produced within the last 5–7 years.

Do not simply do a close reading of the "text"; instead, situate your analysis in its cultural context: time, place, political or social climate, as an artistic production, as a consumer product, etc. To add analytical depth, be sure to use *theories or concepts* drawn from at least *3 of our course readings*. Feel free, as well, to reference other sources (reviews, interviews, news articles, etc.) as they help you support your points. Be sure to include a *Works Cited page* on which you reference all material cited in your text (following MLA format for in-text and final citations). Be careful to avoid a paper that slips into one long summary. Provide summary only to briefly remind your readers of the artifact and when necessary to support your analytical points. This is not about getting the "right" or "true" interpretation of the text; instead, consider yourself contributing to the wider conversation about the text/artifact.

12.2   *Locating a Text/Artifact for Analysis*
- Brainstorm recent movies/series with explicit or implicit themes of whiteness: *The Free State of Jones, Loving, When They See Us,* Disney movies, etc. The movie does not have to overtly deal with race.
- Brainstorm t.v. shows (reality, comedy, news, etc.): cop shows, a decorating show, coverage of protests/demonstrations, *(Fear) The Walking Dead, Law and Order, Orange is the New Black, Scandal,* etc.
- Look around on YouTube.
- Brainstorm recent songs, videos, or albums: Macklemore's work or a recent performance, Brad Paisley's "Accidental Racist," Josh Turner's "White Boys," portrayals of whiteness in videos by musicians of color.
- Musical or Plays: *Avenue Q.*
- Art, Statues, Brochures, Military Posters, billboards, etc.

12.3   *Style and Conventions*
Your tone and voice should be appropriate for your subject matter and your academic audience. Remember, academic audiences do not appreciate a writer's use of sexist, racist, classist, or other oppressive discourse. You should also strive to produce stylistically savvy prose. That is, your analysis should be an engaging read. Avoid overgeneralizations; you aren't "proving" anything; instead, you hope to get your audience to give at least some serious consideration to your points. Furthermore, your text should also be grammatically correct and (given the expectations of a college audience) written in standard, edited English. After revising for content development, be sure to take the final steps of editing and proofreading to better insure your credibility and a positive audience reception. Further review MLA format for integrating quotes and paraphrases into your text and for coordinating these with a Works Cited page.

12.4 *Organization*

Analysis goes beyond summary and description to look beyond the surface.

The introduction:
- Catches readers' attention and/or helps readers understand why they might be interested in or care about your topic
- Introduces the text, the title, the genre, the author, and the context (magazine, time period, etc.) in which the artifact originally appeared/was published
- Gives your thesis outright or strongly indicates the direction in which your analytical argument is headed

Subsequent paragraph: Depending upon how familiar you imagine your audience is with the artifact you're analyzing, you may need to have a brief summary paragraph. If you don't have a single summary paragraph, be sure not to make your whole essay simply a summary.

Body paragraphs (note: this is plural; there should be several body paragraphs): Each body paragraph is focused around a feature for analysis. Often, the topic sentence is stated outright; in the case of an implied topic sentence, the paragraph should still focus on a single feature. After providing a transition or topic sentence, the entire paragraph is devoted to providing supporting evidence for the analytical claim you are forwarding: here, your points will center around production, circulation, reception, and other rhetorical appeals. This evidence can come from references to the text, quotes from interviews, quotes from reviews, etc. Consider ending paragraphs with wrap up sentences to remind your readers of the point behind your analysis/the tie-in to your larger thesis.

Production: Who produced this text? What was their aim? What social, cultural, political, artistic forces prompted them to produce the text?

Circulation: How do various groups come into contact with the text? Where did it originally appear? How has it been re- or unofficially circulated? What do the sites of circulation/encounter say about the intended audiences or how others have appropriated the text?

Reception: How do the producers want folks to respond? How have different groups responded (buying the product, being offended, protesting against it, making fun of it, etc.)? What do different responses say about how the text is functioning in the re-presentation of race/whiteness in American (or other) culture?

Conclusion: Avoid simply repeating or paraphrasing all of your main points. Sometimes, it is useful to restate the title/artifact. Be sure to draw larger implications for your analysis. That is, remind your audience of the larger purpose or the so-what of your analysis: why should we care or how does this matter?

Practice being an engaging writer, yourself, by ending on a strong, rather than flat or tired, note.

12.5   *Evaluation*

Your texts will be evaluated based upon the focus, depth, and credibility of your analysis. Have you provided enough evidence and support to convince your audience that the text represents whiteness in the ways you claim? Does your organization make sense and lead your readers through your analysis? Are your tone and ethos well enough established to garner readers' trust in your analysis (we don't have to agree, but we do need to feel like what you're saying has some merit for consideration)? Are ideas well developed? Have you considered any important counter-claims that your audience might well be familiar with? Is your prose readable, engaging, and/or even sophisticated? Have you taken care to edit and proofread so that readers remain focused on your ideas? Have you correctly followed MLA format for in-text citations and for your Works Cited page?

13   Sample Cultural Studies Rhetorical Analysis

The Power Struggle Paradox
Whiteness vs Monstrosity in The Powerpuff Girls

Daniel Giraldo & Elaine Ruby Gunn

"Sugar, spice, and everything nice. These were the ingredients chosen to create the perfect little girl. But Professor Utonium accidentally added an extra ingredient to the concoction: Chemical X! Thus the Powerpuff Girls were born! Using their ultra superpowers, Blossom, Bubbles, and Buttercup have dedicated their lives to fighting crime and the forces of evil!"

The Powerpuff Girls, Opening Sequence Narration

∴

Introduction

On September 17, 2017, Season 2 of the 2016 *Powerpuff Girls* series-reboot aired on Cartoon Network, as a five-part event named *The Power of Four*. Originally created by animator Craig McCracken, the program was produced by Hanna-Barbera until 2001 when Cartoon Network Studios took over production. Nearly twenty years after the Emmy award-winning, animated TV-series made its network debut, *The Powerpuff Girls* (PPG), featuring three kindergarten-aged, super-powered, white little girls—and their battles against a series of evil, *monstrous* villains—get a sister. But, not just any sister. According to the reboot event's narrative, ten years before Professor Utonium made the infamous Powerpuff Girls, he had performed another science experiment to create the *perfect little girl*. In both the original series and the reboot event, the Professor uses the same ingredients but with slight variation. In the original series, the Girls were created with Chemical X, as noted in the opening sequence narration above. However, in the reboot, which became the Professor's earliest attempt at what he thought to be the perfect little girl, he used Chemical W to make Bliss—short for Blisstina Francesca Francia Mariam Alicia Utonium. The Professor's pioneering attempt at creating a daughter was not only a flawed one, according to the show, but it also made Bliss unstable. Aside from marking Bliss as different than Blossom, Bubbles, and Buttercup, clearly Chemicals X and W are also made up of Othering components that can be best observed through the lens of *whiteness* theory.

FIGURE 6.1
The Power of Four

In an article written by Thomas Ross, titled "White Innocence, Black Abstraction," he credits a recent commentator on the topic of how twentieth-century psychoanalysts have suggested that blackness can be associated with repressed libidinous impulses (262): "Carl Gustav Jung has even argued that the Negro became for European whites a symbol of the unconscious itself—of what he calls 'the shadow'—the whole suppressed or rejected side of the human psyche" (Ross 262). In terms of the PPG, Bliss is, too, such a *shadow*—made explicitly into a person of color (POC) for the show—not only in terms of her demonstrated mind powers, but also of one that denotes progress towards *perfection* via implicit juxtaposition to the embodied whiteness of the Girls.

This connection is made most evident through Ross' explanation of how white innocence works as a special rhetorical device. He states that "when the contemporary rhetoric of white innocence invites the cultural connections and images, we may be tapping into a repressed vein of unconscious racism which cannot be expressed in any way but indirectly and metaphorically" (Ross 264). The Girls are the epitome of white innocence, and what follows is not only a closer examination of the indirect (and often metaphorical) racism portrayed in the popular children's television show, but it also contains an exposition of how this cartoon contributes to Margaret M. Russell's definition of the dominant gaze—that is, "the tendency of mainstream culture to replicate, through narrative and imagery, racial inequalities and biases which exist throughout society" (163).

A conflicting rhetorical device with that of white innocence is that of *monstrosity*. As presented in the article "On the Cover of Rolling Stone: Deconstructing Monsters and Terrorism in an Era of Post Racial Whiteness," Leda Cooks argues that monsters are not antithetical to whiteness. In fact, she affirms that they are "constitutive of white identities" (Cooks 202). Therefore, the *monsters* in the PPG universe, and the Other identities they embody, ultimately serve as a reflection of a white, embedded narrative within our popular culture. While it may not have been McCracken's intentions for the show to exhibit racism thusly, its effects cast Others in a ghastly light—one that further promotes whiteness as the norm.

Thus, considering the reboot's addition of a fourth girl to the cast—this time a POC—this paper performs: i) a rhetorical analysis of the dominant hegemonic power structures in the PPG universe, while ii) considering how the monsters, who represent an abstracted conglomerate of white racist fears, are products of their whitewashed environment who serve to further entrench whiteness as the foundation for an equality "based on the perceived value of merit, hard work, and cultural imperialism" (Cooks 206).

Background

Four years after the series made its official debut, *The Powerpuff Girls Movie* was released in theaters, on July 3, 2002, by Warner Bros. Family Entertainment. The film was featured as a prequel to the series, accounting for the Girls' origins and their progression into becoming the defenders of Townsville. As part of the film's plot, Professor Utonium hopes to improve the city of Townsville that is plagued by crime and injustice. He acts on his optimism by creating the perfect little girls to inherit knowledge of good and evil.

This sequence is already problematic for the reboot event's plot, as noted by several critics. Knowing that Bliss (the fourth/first PPG) was the Professor's original attempt at creating the perfect little girl, viewers are left with an indirect replication of racial inequality; with a syllogism that steps logically towards "white, perfect Powerpuff Girls" as stated by Suprihmbé. The self-proclaimed "proheaux womanist thot scholar," questions the producers' decision for including a POC in the reboot event, declaring: "if representation is important, then give us a Bliss who isn't the result of an irresponsible white man." Writer Charles Pulliam-Moore, of *Gizmodo*, also doubts whether the reboot event was a good idea, stating: "Bliss is coded as a person of color. Everything about Bliss is designed to set her apart from the three original Powerpuff Girls... Bliss reads as distinctly non-white and decidedly multi-ethnic."

Danielle Ransom, a writer for *The Daily Dot*, validates Pulliam-Moore's skepticism of the reboot, regarding the event as "a missed opportunity to address her race at all"—one made from a colorblind perspective. "Many fans were nonplussed with Bliss being portrayed as a stereotype of an angry Black girl," Ransom continues. Citing an *Essence* report, from 2013, that found Black women to be "commonly surrounded by negative depictions twice as often as positive depictions," she notes that Bliss was "an opportunity to directly address a demographic that often sees themselves represented as mammies, sexually deviants, and unfit mothers." Rather than contributing to a critical race dialogue, the consensus among many of the show's viewers and critics are roughly the same— that is, the producer's efforts at diversity were instead the effects of mere tokenism.

FIGURE 6.2
Professor Utonium

In order to understand why the producers included a POC into a show of predominantly whitewashed values, it is necessary to briefly review the society within which the Girls reside. The aforementioned critics raise several valid points in challenging Bliss' genesis, but ultimately, their comments do not contribute to an understanding of the whiteness problem: an issue that is concealed inconspicuously in the PPG background. As the source of the Girls' civic pride and power, for instance, Professor Utonium is the embodiment of what sociologists and whiteness theory scholars identify as a WASP. The acronym, when broken apart, is: *white, Anglo-Saxon, male*. Throughout the film and the show, the Professor frequently portrays the quintessential traits of conscience, industry, success, civic-mindedness, use and anti-sensuality: the traits enumerated in Richard Brookhiser's work titled, "The Way of the Wasp." But rather than provide examples of how the Professor exemplifies these traits, or how he indoctrinates the Girls with them, labeling the Professor as such provides a lens through which to view him and other white archetypes in the context of the PPG universe.

Like most laboratories, the Professor's is a sterile, white space. This motif extends outward from his lab into the rest of his home, his neighborhood, and his city. His position of authority, as a scientist, over the people of Townsville, is that of black absence (made especially apparent by Bliss and the reboot event), suggesting that only whiteness, e.g. the intelligence afforded to whites, is the city's saving grace. The Professor lives in a noticeably suburban neighborhood, in a city run by white people in positions of power, all of whom are oblivious to the city's socioeconomic problems. For example, after the Mayor's initial interaction with the Girls in the film—they leave most of the city in ruins after a simple game of tag, ending with the destruction of the Mayor's favorite pickle stand—is demonstrative of white privilege, as his only preoccupation is no longer having a physical location where he can purchase a pickle. Another example comes after the Professor is incarcerated having been blamed for the destruction of Townsville due to the Girls' game of tag. His only concerns are for the Girls' white innocence: "What if they're cold, or hungry? How will they find their way home?" he asks, after forbidding them to fly or use their powers outside the home.

FIGURE 6.3   Townsville

In short, the Professor and the Mayor, representative pillars of whiteness, both "operate from a sphere of whiteness," inhibiting their ability to see the negative effects of whiteness, unless its effects inconvenience them (DeRouen and Grant 59). This blatant white-blindness is an interesting parallel to Ransom's article in *The Daily Dot*. Returning to the case of Bliss, Ransom states that *color*blindness is (counter)productive:

> In many ways, the Powerpuff writers' approach to Bliss feels more like an attempt to hop on diversity trends like #blackgirlmagic and #melaninonfleek without bothering to develop a well-rounded character. It's a poor attempt at fitting in (and cashing in) on black empowerment movements without doing the sensitive, thought-through work... A fuller characterization of Bliss that encompasses her racial identity

would let Black children know that it matters that they're represented. It would make them feel seen and understood, instead of just reminding them that society marks them as an "other" with wild emotions and large hips.

For a modern cartoon to be circulated for juvenile entertainment without taking race into consideration beyond stereotypes and tokenism is arguably irresponsible. And it begs the question: was Bliss included in the reboot event to counter the pervasive whiteness throughout the PPG universe, or is her presence indicative of how the PPGs are operating within a mode of colorblindness? Regardless, as the show is broadcast from within a white society, we are reminded of how discourse objects emerge conceptually out of Foucauldian surfaces. The ideas held by white identities, and their definitions of the Other, thus proliferate out from a seat of power that is deeply entrenched by a white agenda, even throughout a medium as *innocent* as the PPG. Ultimately, and perhaps without intention, the PPGs and its creators perpetuate portrayals of Others that are delimited by white racist fears. Thus, the discourse objects that emerge from our society and from the PPG universe are one in the same. And it is precisely the Other, superimposed upon a background of whiteness, that reveals how minority presence functions rhetorically within the series, and how monstrosity is constitutive of white normativity.

Foreground

Most of the villains in the PPG universe are overt, stereotypical representations of the Other from a white racist perspective. They are various embodiments of *monsters,* as the term applies to whiteness studies. Let us recall how these Others, or monsters, are constitutive of white identities, particularly the white innocence/white savior identities incorporated within the PPG series. This monstrous rhetorical device ultimately reflects both the whiteness and racism exhibited throughout the show.

The Girls' first villain is comprised of at least three distinct ethnicities, that of Asian, Middle Eastern, and African American descent. At first glance, Mojo Jojo is an evil, *monstrous* monkey with an inferiority complex who vaguely represents an amalgamation of several minorities. Though, through a deeper look at Jojo's roots, we can observe how he is a product of the whiteness inherent within the PPG series.

FIGURE 6.4   Mojo Jojo

Historically, African Americans have been reduced to animals, often disparagingly as *apes* or *monkeys*. If it were not for the pervasive whiteness throughout the series, Mojo Jojo would be just another primate: a non-racial construct, acting as both a protagonist and antagonist, at separate times, like King Kong. However, the phonemic patterns and enunciated vowels in Jojo's name and speech resemble that of Eastern/Asian languages. His "brain cover" also resembles that of a turban typically worn in the Middle East. He is, as Anna Everett expresses in her rhetorical study of racial cinematic patterns, a preconditioned narrative "on a racialized character hierarchy" (34). Having aired less than a year after the attacks on the World Trade Center, the PPGs' main villain may very well be a subconscious, dramatic response to the rapid increase in racial skepticism and paranoia spreading throughout the United States. The exigent Otherness of Mojo Jojo is shaped by this emphasis on violence and terrorist activity in the media during the early 2000s.

Jojo's origins, however, as told through the first PPG film, reveal his monstrosity to be a direct result of intentional whiteness at work in the PPG society. The first time the Girls meet Jojo—his name before becoming the known villain Mojo Jojo—he saves them from the Gangreen Gang: a squad of grotesque, teenage-looking villains. The Girls are attacked by the Gang only after entering into the *trashy*, urbanized parts of the city that work in contrast to the Girls' white innocence. Upon thanking Jojo for coming to their aid, he speaks the following to them:

> I dare not listen for I have been lashed by harsh tongues for too long. Alas, my little ones, I do not rock, for I, Jojo, am a monster...My pain is not for you to understand. Besides, how could you? For you are pure and innocent and most certainly loved. How could you know what it is to be cast out into a world that only offers misery? How could you know what it's like for people to fear you and despise you for the very things that make you special, because you don't fit in, because you are a freak.

The Girls' response and attempt at relating to Jojo's pain speaks to how white innocence is oblivious to the experiential Other, as noted by Christine Farris. She argues how "stereotypes typically remain intact" within "popular representations of collective pain and supposed transcendence of racism" (46). We may observe that, even though Jojo and the Girls may share some level of pain related to their exclusion, the racial Other is depicted as dependent, manipulative, and dangerous. In contrast, however, the Girls' innocence is exemplary of what Peggy Mcintosh describes as *elusive* and *fugitive*. In her essay titled "White Privilege: Unpacking the Invisible Knapsack," Mcintosh continues her work of introspection stating that "power from unearned privilege can look like strength when it is in fact permission to escape or to dominate" (6). For the Girls, their power stems from unearned *white* privilege and it allows them and their white counterparts to retreat behind their whiteness. These qualities are not only infused into the Girls' DNA by the Professor, but it is also colored by the cartoonists, themselves. In essence, the Girls—together with that of their physical and metaphysical creators—are oblivious to the fact that they are products of the problem itself. They are products of whiteness.

Middle-ground

Though less overt, and perhaps part of an unintentional narrative, whites serve as the prime monsters to both themselves and to marginalized groups within the PPG universe. bell hooks describes this whiteness as a kind of terrorism in which whites are "oblivious to their own visibility as monsters" (Cooks 205). After an intense game of tag, for example, the Girls leave the city of Townsville in shambles: cars are crashed, people are maimed, and buildings are burned to the ground. The Professor's unapologetic response to the destroyed town not only demonstrates his blinding white privilege, but also reveals his "terrorizing imposition," as hooks would describe, towards the Other citizens of Townsville (qtd. in Cooks 205). "'They do not imagine that the way whiteness makes its presence felt, most often as terrorizing imposition, is a power that wounds, hurts, tortures, is a reality that disrupts the fantasy of whiteness as representing goodness'" (qtd. in Cooks 205). In the PPG film, the Professor and the Mayor are blinded to the fact that they and the Girls operate as monsters. But, at several instances throughout the PPG television series, whiteness briefly seems to lose its monstrosity. Instead, the focus is redirected toward marginal groups that work to obscure and confound the dominant hegemonic power structures in the PPG universe.

For instance, in the season 5 episode titled "Save Mojo," Mojo Jojo takes advantage of the white savior, despite its polysemous function as the white oppressor. Martha Southgate helps clarify the oxymoronic existence of the white savior: a trope "'that a particular white character is somehow crucial or even necessary'" to any tale of liberation (qtd. in Farris 43). An example of this comes from a scene where Mojo Jojo whines (literally) about how he is being oppressed by the Townsville elites. He is immediately consoled by at least five white citizens, all of whom embody the Social Justice Warrior (SJW) stereotype. Here, we return to Cooks for further explanation of the modern monster as an embodiment of both exterior and interior differences (203). As Mojo Jojo's only advocates, these SJWs serve as a combination of both Southgate's and Cook's analyses and act in direct opposition to the Girls since they are the protagonists. While the SJWs are whites, they are "less white" because of their support for the marginalized. In effect, their activism, particularly for Mojo Jojo (i.e. minorities), is portrayed as irrelevant, villainous, and detrimental to society.

Another example of observed middle-ground can be examined in the first season of the PPG series. Fuzzy Lumpkins, another villain, is introduced by the series' narrator as someone "[who has] decided to be far, far away; [someone who doesn't] like visitors." The angle used in the viewer's approach to Lumpkins is similar to that of a nature documentary, as the narrator recounts how Lumpkins is akin to an unapproachable animal. Holding a shotgun and sitting in a rocker next to a jug filled with moonshine, Lumpkins represents the underprivileged white man, i.e., white trash. According to rhetoricians Jennifer Beech and Matthew Guy, this series of successive images within a film—which furthers the Othering characterization of the

PPG monsters—is a *suture*, or the way in which the observer of a film creates cohesiveness of narrative (157). Lumpkins' hillbilly persona is in drastic contrast to Brookhiser's rendition of the WASP. In this case the Professor, the Mayor, and the Girls, can be *more* white than the *white trash* embodied by Lumpkins. This notion of a whiteness hierarchy implies that there is a pedigree among whites (DeRouen and Grant 58). Fuzzy Lumpkins—a play on words to sounds like the phrase *country bumpkin*—is depicted as overweight, uneducated, and territorial, insinuating that the poor, those outside of the white-washed suburbia of Townsville, have ostracized and voluntarily marginalized themselves.

Lastly, HIM, the over-sexualized demonic villain, is illustrative of a cross dresser, something unfound in any other character in the PPG universe. His effeminate nature—comprised of a tutu, a set of high heels, and a face of exaggerated make-up—creates a queer Other, an abhorrent contradiction to the white heteronormative. He is introduced in the season 1 episode, "Octi Evil," as a villain "so evil, so sinister, so horribly vile that even the utterance of his name strikes fear into the hearts of men!" He is ostracized by the Townsvillagers and takes solace in his home, the Underworld, emerging only to do damage to the town. Such a demeaning description falls in line with Cooks' claim that "white-identified people ask for conformity to the norm before the recognition of equality" (206). In other words, it is not only HIM's villainy that marginalizes him, but his girly demeanor and homosexual candor that conflict with the heteronormative motif, ultimately rendering him unsafe. If the racial, socioeconomic, and sexual Others have been characterized so blatantly by the series' creators, it is hard to assume this perceived racism was unintentional by the PPG writers, producers, and directors.

Conclusion

In closing, the dominant hegemonic power structures in the PPG universe can be brought into focus through a critical lens of whiteness studies, providing an observation of the intentionally explicit and unintentionally implicit monstrosities within both the series and film. Tokenized characters like Bliss, and misinformed conceptions of the marginalized like Mojo Jojo, "threaten the stability of society" and work in contrast to responsible racial representation (Cooks 212). Regardless of the producers' intentions, the manipulation of the hackneyed stereotypes used to reinforce concepts of danger has affected a racialized PPG audience.

Whiteness, however, reflected in our society through pop-cultural depictions made evident throughout Townsville, serves as the unequivocal villain. "For [bell] hooks," Cooks notes, "whiteness works as terrorism, as a kind of monster for those defined as marginal or invisible within its histories, literatures, institutions and in its daily practices" (212). Surely, such monsters are to be feared on screen by a white-blinded audience; however, the true monstrosity exists in the thoughtless promotion of manifested discriminatory material. The longer the biases implicit to whiteness go unnoticed, especially in realms as improvident as entertainment, the greater the field of perceived monstrosity will grow. Monsters only become Othered through a narrowed, dominant gaze. The paradoxical power struggles of whiteness against monstrosity within the PPG universe are also our own.

Works Cited

Beech, Jennifer A. and Matthew Guy. "Rick Grimes, Eastman, and White Power: Resisting the Suture from a Critical Fan Perspective." *The Walking Dead Live! Essays on the Television Show*, edited by Philip L. Simpson and Marcus Mallard, Rowman and Littlefield, 2016, pp. 155–164.

Brookhiser, Richard. "The Way of the WASP." *Critical Whiteness Studies: Looking Behind the Mirror*, edited by Richard Delgado and Jean Stefanic, Temple UP, 1997, pp. 6–11.

Cooks, Leda. "On the Cover of the Rolling Stone: Deconstructing Monsters and Terrorism in an Era of Postracial Whiteness." Kennedy et al., pp. 201–221.

DeRouen, Anita and M. Shane Grant. "Mus(n't) See TV: Hidden Whiteness in Representations of Women of Color." Kennedy et al., pp. 54–70.

Everett, Anna. "The Other Pleasures: The Narrative Function of Race in the Cinema." *Film Criticism*, vol. 20, no. 1/2, 1995, pp. 26–38.

Kennedy, Tammie M., et. al., editors. *Rhetorics of Whiteness: Postracial Hauntings in Popular Culture, Social Media, and Education*, Southern Illinois UP, 2017.

McIntosh, Peggy. "White Privilege: Unpacking the Invisible Knapsack." 1989. PDF.

"Octi Evil." *The Powerpuff Girls*, written by Kevin Kaliher, directed by Genndy Tartakovsky and Craig McCracken, Cartoon Network, 1998.

The Powerpuff Girls Movie. Directed by Craig McCracken, performances by Cathy Cavadini, Tara Strong, and Elizabeth Daily, Warner Bros. Family Entertainment, 2002.

Pulliam-Moore, Charles. "Bliss, the New Powerpuff Girl, Deserved a Much Better Story Than The Power of Four." *io9*, io9.Gizmodo.com, 18 Sept. 2017, io9.gizmodo.com/bliss-the-new-powerpuff-girl-deserved-a-much-better-s-1818506002. Accessed 18 Nov. 2017.

Ransom, Danielle. "The New Dark-Skinned Powerpuff Girl Is Little More than a Token." *The Daily Dot*, 22 Sept. 2017, www.dailydot.com/irl/new-black-powerpuff-girl/. Accessed 18 Nov. 2017.

Ross, Thomas. "White Innocence, Black Abstraction." *Critical White Studies: Looking behind the Mirror*, Temple UP, 1997, pp. 263–265.

Russell, Margaret M. "Race and the Dominant Gaze: Narratives of Law and Inequality in Popular Film," *Legal Studies Forum*, vol. 15, no. 3, 1991, pp. 243–254.

"Save Mojo." *The Powerpuff Girls*, written by Greg Colton, directed by Randy Myers, Cartoon Network, 2003.

Suprihmbé. "Powerpuff Girl Bliss Presents a Familiar Mirror of Scientific Abuse of Black Women." *Wear Your Voice*, 23 Sept. 2017, wearyourvoicemag.com/identities/race/powerpuff-girl-bliss-presents-familiar-mirror-scientific-abuse-black-women. Accessed 18 Nov. 2017.

Glossary

Affirmative action A set of laws, guidelines, policies, and procedures intended to prevent discrimination or to address past discrimination against non-dominant groups. In the United States, President John F. Kennedy signed Executive Order 10925, which committed government contractors to "take affirmative action to ensure that applicants are employed, and employees are treated during employment, without regard to their race, creed, color, or national origin." President Lyndon B. Johnson's Executive Order 11246, which was amended in 1967 to include sex, superseded that previous order and applied to all federal contractors and subcontractors. Further acts that have promoted affirmative action policies are as follows: Equal Pay Act of 1963; Title VII of the Civil Rights Act of 1964 (race, color, religion, national origin); Age Discrimination Act of 1973, Rehabilitation Act of 1973 (people with disabilities); Americans with Disabilities Act of 1990; the Civil Rights Act of 1991; and the Boy Scouts of America Equal Access Act (as amended in 2001 by the No Child Left Behind Act, to allow access by community groups to school facilities during non-school hours). Educational institutions receiving federal funds must document their affirmative action policies, and special scrutiny is paid to institutions that have in the past enacted discriminatory policies. (See the Court Cases section for important cases directly related to Affirmative Action.)

Allyship To position oneself as an ally to another group. This term has especially become associated with white people who act as allies to people of color. The Anti-Oppressive Network (see Web Resources) notes that allyship is a lifelong process, rather than an individual identity, and they provide an excellent handout with tools for acting as an ally. It's important to listen to the cautions and critiques of white allyship offered by people of color, as well as feminist and queer scholars, particularly with respect to the need for white people to avoid adopting a savior mentality with respect to other groups.

Anti-miscegenation laws Laws that criminalized interracial marriage and, sometimes, interracial sex. While in the United States, there never existed a federal ban on interracial marriage, it was not until 1967 that the Supreme Court ruled—in Loving v. Virginia—unconstitutional these anti-miscegenation laws. At that time, sixteen states still had such laws on their books. In 2000, Alabama became the last state to officially legalize interracial marriage.

Anti-semitism Open or subconscious hostility towards or prejudice against Jews, often resulting in stereotyping and acts of violence.

Assimilation The process of a non-dominant group or immigrant minority taking on the habits, lifestyles, attitudes, and other norms of the dominant group or host culture. Full assimilation comes at the cost of losing one's original culture. It is worth noting, as well, that some non-dominant groups are often denied assimilation by the hegemonic group.

Binarism A social and legal construct that positions things in terms of the false dichotomy of black/white.

Black abstraction A rhetorical construct and central tenant of nineteenth-century jurisprudence that essentially placed blacks as existing outside of any real social/human context. By denying the humanness of blacks, whites could justify the subjugation of African-Americans. (See Thomas Ross "White Innocence, Black Abstraction" and "The Rhetorical Tapestry of Race.")

Color blindness The faulty premise that ignoring or supposedly not seeing race abolishes racism and structural inequality or makes one free of racism. Color blindness is also used in business and legal practices as a way of claiming to make race-free decisions, hence ignoring implicit biases and structural racism. White people in particular, who are less likely to have received discriminatory treatment due to their race, are apt to claim to be color blind.

Cultural appropriation Oppressive and unethical use of aspects of someone else's culture (art, cultural practices, icons, music, food, etc.). This is especially problematic when a member of a dominant group takes on a practice or claims to have invented a cultural practice of a non-dominant group. (Examples: white fraternity members engaging in the traditionally African-American practice of stepping; use or reproduction (for sale) of instruments, icons, or religious practices of indigenous peoples for mere fun or decoration; wearing dreadlocks, mohawks, or cornrows as mere fashion without effort to understand the traditions behind those hair styles and/or no attempt to act as allies for oppressed groups.)

De jure v. de facto (for segregation and discrimination). While initially many practices were by law (*de jure*), even after Jim Crow and other racist laws were reversed, communities, institutions, and individuals often still implemented *de facto* (by practice) discrimination and segregation.

Discourse of resentment The practice of defining one's identity through a negation of the other; most often, this term is used to describe both individuals and systems designed to pit the dominant group against non-dominant groups. (See "Oppositional identity" for when a non-dominant group forms its identity in direct contrast to the dominant group.) Pop culture, the media, and various propaganda outlets feed a discourse of resentment against the poor, those on social programs, feminist groups, immigrants, people in inner cities, etc., so that the resentment type personality (see Nietzsche's 1967 *Genealogy of Morals*) often defines himself against an other with whom he has had little to no contact.

Dog whistle politics Much like a dog can hear sounds at a certain pitch not audible to the human ear, dog whistles in political discourse refer to coded messages that are often perceived by the general public as being innocent, while simultaneously sending other—usually, racist, classist, sexist, homophobic, etc.—messages to those readily able and willing to decode them. For instance, when Rick Tyler from Tennessee ran for Congress, he decoded another candidate's dog whistle and cut to the chase by erecting a billboard that read "Make America White Again." An older example would be Ronald Reagan's continued reference to "welfare queens." A pervasive example would be references to the Civil War as being about "states' rights."

Environmental racism A systemic form of racism whereby toxins and environmental hazards are introduced in or near communities largely occupied by people of color and indigenous people. Think: Detroit's water pollution; pipelines running above/near the water supplies of Native-Americans.

Epistemic violence Modes of knowing enacted by the dominant group to rationalize domination and/or to provide a purposefully or unself-reflectively limited interpretation of data on "others." Think, the pseudo-science of eugenics; think, legal constructs that forwarded black abstraction (i.e., saw blacks as non-human).

Ethnicity An association with a group based upon sharing a certain culture, set of traditions and beliefs, linguistic patterns, religious practices, etc.

Ethnocentrism Preferring one's culture and ethnicity and judging other cultures against the standards of one's own culture.

Eugenics Pseudo-scientific belief in the ability to improve the human race genetically through such practices as selective breeding, sterilization or racial genocide of "undesirable" populations, and other means of manipulating DNA. Beliefs about being well born or from good stock date back to ancient Greece, but it was Francis Galton who coined the term in 1883. During the Nuremberg trials, German defendants attempted to excuse their gross human rights violations as attempts at eugenics. At the turn of the twentieth century, the U.S. Eugenics Records Office attempted to claim that rural poor whites were genetically defective, supposedly due to racial mixing at some point in the family history. The beliefs operating behind this pseudo-science are generally considered racist and unethical.

First Nations, Indigenous peoples, Native Americans Term referring to people who have occupied North America prior to and after invasion/colonization/inhabitation of Europeans. Indigenous peoples of Canada are often referred to as First Nation, whereas, Native Americans is the term often employed in the U.S.

Gerrymandering Purposefully drawing the boundaries of a voting district to influence the outcome towards a particular party or race. Racial gerrymandering has been in effect from the Reconstruction Era on. Often, in order to prevent a racial minority from electing their preferred candidate, the party in power will redraw voting districts to split up the votes of people in a particular neighborhood—sometimes even people living on the same street. As recently as June 2019, the U.S. Supreme Court upheld findings that Virginia's House Republicans had redrawn voting districts in ways that prevented African-Americans from electing their chosen candidates.

Hegemony/hegemonic group   A position of cultural and political dominance; the dominant group; sometimes called the majority (although this can be misleading because the numerical majority may not be the group that is on a position of dominance).

Immigrant minority v. involuntary minority   These terms were coined by John Ogbu to distinguish between people who come to a country voluntarily for improved economic and other opportunities versus those who were brought through slavery, conquest, or colonization. Immigrant minorities often have ties to kin in their country of origin and are better able to practice "accommodation without assimilation" or to play the assimilation game; they are often seen as so-called "model minorities." Involuntary minorities tend to be viewed by the hegemonic culture as inferior or undesirable, and in turn, they tend to view whites and white culture unfavorably, not wishing to assimilate; often, assimilation is denied to them—both systemically and subconsciously on the part of the dominant group.

Implicit bias   Attitudes or feelings towards a group that are unacknowledged or that operate beyond a person's awareness or consciousness.

Intersectionality   Intersectional theories generally acknowledge that we all simultaneously occupy multiple and often competing subjectivities and that social pressures often make us feel compelled to align ourselves with one subjectivity in ways that work against our own self-interest. For instance, women of color often feel pressured to align themselves with their race, as opposed with a feminist agenda. Different waves of feminism have come under critique for failing to attend to the material conditions of working-class women and women of color in general. Working-class whites often trade class solidarity for race privilege. Intersectional theorists call upon us to recognize our complexity and interconnectedness and particularly to recognize that we cannot fight for the rights of any group at the exclusion of other non-dominant groups.

Jim Crow Laws   State and local laws (put in place in Southern states in the late 19th and early 20th centuries) designed to enforce racial segregation. Think: segregation in public schools and in public restrooms; requiring African-Americans to sit in the back seats of public transportation.

Manifest destiny   A nineteenth-century belief that God destined the United States for westward territorial expansion. This belief was often invoked to justify the obliteration of indigenous peoples.

Neoliberalism   An ideology emphasizing free market capitalism, valuing competition over regulation, defining citizens as consumers and as agents of their own free will, and championing the privatization of social institutions. In the United States, neoliberalism is associated with economic policies begun during the Reagan era, especially the reduction or elimination of programs designed to provide a social safety net. During the Trump era, we can observe neoliberalism at work through school voucher programs and efforts to privatize schools, deregulation of industries with respect to environmental standards and consumer protections, deregulation of business and finance, anti-unionism, privatization of public lands, among myriad other policies. Neoliberal policies are often put forth as supposedly normal, neutral, or common sense when in reality they mask systemic racism and oppressive heteronormativity, as well as other sexist and ableist hierarchal regimes.

One-drop rule   (also called hypo-descent rule and traceable amount rule). In the United States, this was a social and legal practice for classifying someone's race, particularly for classifying someone as black based upon the belief that if a person had one black ancestor or one "drop of black blood," that person was black. Hypo-descent or percentage rules varied from state to state and were used to keep African-Americans in slavery, from having legal rights (to freedom, to marry whom they wished, to vote, etc.), and from entry into social and other institutions (churches, clubs, schools, etc.). These laws also allowed for white masters to rape their slaves, while disallowing their offspring to claim to be white or to be entitled to rights accorded to whites.

Oppositional identity   Another term coined by John Ogbu to describe how members of non-dominant groups—especially those he terms involuntary minorities—define themselves in opposition to the dominant culture. Involuntary minorities—according to Ogbu—tend to view assimilation as a form of selling out, or they simply recognize the unwillingness of the dominant group to allow them to assimilate even when they desire to.

Oxymoronic Whiteness   A term explicated by Kennedy, Middleton, and Ratcliffe in *Rhetorics of Whiteness* that is useful for moving beyond false binaries with respect to discussions and interrogations of whiteness. Rather than thinking in terms that place one as white/not white, racist/not racist, or willing/not willing to examine or discuss whiteness, "Imagining whiteness as an oxymoron, however, invites us to identify multiple contradictions in discursive uses of whiteness, whether the term is directly employed or serves as a haunting." Oxymoronic whiteness is helping for interrogating how the term white is used outright or through dog whistles in public and private discussions, as well as for critiquing those who see themselves as white allies for people of color.

People of color v. colored people The terms colored (in the U.S.) and coloureds (U.K., South Africa) were especially used in times of apartheid and Jim Crow eras as ways to pejoratively mark people of African descent as non-white. While groups like the NAACP adopted the usage, activists like Malcolm X rejected terms like "colored" and "negro" in favor of describing people as black. In the late 1980's, activists began to use "people of color" as a way to denote someone who is not white or someone who is of a mixed racial background. People of color—like "people with disabilities"—uses person-first language as a way to denote that a person is more complex than a single descriptor. Generally, critical race theorists advocate calling people what they wish to be called, yet they also warn that such descriptors can be coopted by the dominant culture—as in recent moves to describe rich people as "people with means."

Phenotypically white A term used to describe people who have skin color and features that are perceived to be characteristically white or Caucasian. Some early state laws that had depended upon scopic views of race (the supposed ability to imagined read someone's race by their visually perceived traits) were problematized when people of color were able to pass as "white." It was at this point that many states adopted hypodescent rules (see "One-drop rule").

Race traitor Originally a pejorative term assigned to someone whose attitudes and positions are perceived to be against the interests of their supposed race. The term has been supported by those participating in the New Abolition Racial Project, who embrace the mantra, "Treason to whiteness is loyalty to humanity." In the inaugural Winter 1993 issue of the journal *Race Traitor*, the opening manifesto, entitled, "Abolish the White Race—By Any Means Necessary," declares the white race as purely a social, rhetorical, and historic construct unsupported by science and designed for the purposes of domination. Their non-violent aim is to dismantle white skin privilege and structures that support white supremacy. A race traitor refuses to collude with white supremacy by, for instance, bearing witness, intervening, and confronting those who tell racist jokes, those who racially profile and harass others, and those whose words, policies, and behaviors oppress people of color.

Racial Bribe, The The process of offering specific racial or ethnic groups certain advantages that come with being classified as "white" in exchange for them helping maintain a white-black divide. When one non-dominant group trades solidarity with others—particularly with other people of color—they are said to have accepted the racial bribe. Such groups have included Irish immigrants (see

Noel Ignatiev's *How the Irish Became White*); Mexican-Americans and other Latinx immigrants (think census coding), as well as Jewish immigrants (see Gunier and Torres' "Whiteness of a Different Color?").

Racial Contract, The In first an essay and then a book by the same name, philosopher Charles W. Mills critiques the social contract theories of Hobbes, Locke, Rousseau, and Kant by pointing out that these philosophers were unable to acknowledge how their own positioning as perceived members of the white race blinded them to how much white supremacy operates as a political system. Race is, according to Mills, the unspoken absent-present of the social contract, the very construct that perpetuates white domination of other races.

Racial homophily To exhibit a preference—whether conscious or not—for associating with people perceived to be of one's same race.

Racial profiling Targeting someone of a particular race or ethnicity for suspicion of having broken the law or committed an offense. Think: stop and frisk; following people of color around in a store for fear that they will shoplift.

Racial stamina A term coined by Robin DiAngelo to describe the ability to live with being uncomfortable when discussing race and with being able to take feedback gratefully. Ideally, someone with racial stamina is better able to combat or avoid white fragility (see the sample review of *White Fragility*).

Racism (as differentiated from bigotry or ethnocentrism) The belief, whether explicit or implicit, in the superiority of one's race—most often from the perspective of the dominant group. Power is key element in differentiating between understanding racism in contrast to bigotry or ethnocentrism. Racist structures operate on power—not simply at an individual level, but also at a structure level. While a person of color may actively dislike a person of another race, their race is not dominant and does not hold power at a structural level, so that person would be said to be bigoted, but their bigotry does not have the power to operate on a large scale to impose its will upon a society. In contrast, a small white boy can call a grown African-American "boy" because larger racist structures have subordinated other races to whites; however, if a person of color calls a white person "cracker," that person might be said to be bigoted, but their act is not racist because it holds no power at a structural level.

Redlining A term for describing racist policies instituted by the Federal Housing Administration in the early 1930's to provide housing for low to middle income whites while simultaneously denying lending or to insure mortgages in African-American neighborhoods. (See Richard Rothstein's *The Color of Law*; also see Adam Ruins Everything "The Disturbing History of the Suburbs.")

"Reverse" racism A false construct that is often used by white people as a term for people of color who exhibit bigoted behavior or for practices that supposedly discriminate against white people (see "Racism").

Rhetorical listening   A concept—fully explicated in Krista Ratcliffe's *Rhetorical Listening: Identifications, Gender, Whiteness*—of listening as a "stance of openness that a person may choose to assume in relation to any person, text, or culture." Ratcliffe identifies three forms of rhetorical listening—listening metonymically, eavesdropping, and listening pedagogically—all with the aim of listening from another's perspective in order to cross cultural boundaries for a deeper understanding and to further the practices of ethical rhetoric.

Rhetorics of whiteness   Rhetoric in general is discourse—written or spoken words, images, art, performance, etc.—designed to change someone's mind, mood, or willingness to act. Rhetorics of whiteness tend to take one of two aims: 1) discourse aimed to critique and resist white supremacy and racist systems; or 2) discourse aimed to reinforce white supremacy and racist systems.

Stereotype threat   Term coined by social psychologists Claude Steele and Joshua Aronson to describe how someone of a stereotyped group fears, internalizes, and/or conforms to a given stereotype. For instance, when women are told they will perform poorly when taking a math test, white sprinters running against black runners, or black males walking through a white neighborhood.

Symbolic violence   Term coined by French sociologist Pierre Bourdieu to describe a type of non-physical violence on the part of a dominant group that is oppressive and can also lead to physical violence against a non-dominant group. For instance, discrimination based upon gender or class; referring to non-standard dialects as "improper" or "wrong," etc.

Whistling Vivaldi   A certain type of defense mechanism—a trope of whiteness—in response to a stereotype threat. Claude Steele describes African-American journalist Brent Staples whistling Vivaldi while walking through white neighborhoods as a way to signal to whites that he was not a threat to white residents.

White fragility   Term coined by Robin DiAngelo now used to refer to the defensiveness displayed and automatic discomfort experienced by many white people when confronted with any type of racial stress, but especially when they are called upon to discuss or acknowledge racism.

White supremacy   The faulty premise that "pure" whites are superior—genetically and otherwise—to other racial groups. Critical race theory and modern genetic science teach us that race is more of a social construct than something biological and call into question notions of pure races. Legal scholars note that the founding fathers forwarded white supremacy in framing our constitution originally only to recognize slaves as 3/5 of a person and by investing property rights in whiteness (see Derrick Bell and Cheryl Harris in Bibliography). Contemporary discourses of white supremacy, as well as white-supremacist behavior, operate at explicit and implicit levels. The Southern Poverty Law Center (see Web Resources) regularly compiles statistics on white nationalist groups (Ku Klux Klan, neo-Confederate, neo-Nazi skinheads, etc.), as well as keeps and publishes a Hatewatch blog to monitor and expose the activities of American white supremacist groups.

White trash   A term thought to originate in the early part of the nineteenth century—sometimes used by black house slaves to refer to poor whites, but more widely adopted by wealthy and now middle-class white people to refer to white people who are poor or who behave in ways supposedly unexpected or unbecoming of whites. The term represents oppressive discourse designed to equate poor whites with human waste. Matt Wray and Annalee Newitz (see Bibliography) trace current stereotypes of white trash to studies produced by the U.S. Eugenics Records Office from 1880–1920, from which the intent was to reason that certain rural whites were poor due to genetic defects.

Whiteness as terror   In contrast to the hegemonic equation of whiteness with innocence and purity (think the virginal white wedding dress), people of color have a long tradition of equating whiteness with terror (think the KKK hoods) (see *Black on White*, ed. David R. Roediger). Note: this does not mean that people of color see white people as terrorists; rather, whiteness as a power structure or an invocation to supremacy is terrifying.

Bibliography

Ahmed, S. (2005). The politics of good feeling. *Australian Journal of Critical Race and Whiteness Studies, 1*(1), 72–85.

Ahmed, S. (2007). A phenomenology of whiteness. *Feminist Theory, 8*(2), 149–168.

Alexander, M. (2012). *The new Jim Crow: Mass incarceration in the age of colorblindness*. The New Press.

Allen, T. W. (1994). *The invention of the White race* (Vol. 1). Verso.

Allen, T. W. (1997). *The invention of the White race* (Vol. 2). Verso.

Anderson, C. (2016). *White rage: The unspoken truth of our racial divide*. Bloomsbury USA.

Applebaum, B. (2013). Vigilance as a response to White complicity. *Educational Theory, 63*(1), 17–34.

Aveling, N. (2006). 'Hacking at our very roots': Rearticulating White racial identity within the context of teacher education. *Race Ethnicity and Education, 9*(3), 261–274.

Baker Jr., H., & Simmons, K. M. (Eds.). (2015). Introduction. In *The trouble with post blackness*. Columbia University Press.

Baldwin, J. (1984). On being 'White' and other lies. *Essence.* 80+.

Biss, E. (2009). Relations. In *Notes from no man's land: American essays*. Graywolf Press.

Biss, E. (2015, December 2). White debt. *The New York Times.* Retrieved from http://www.nytimes.com/2015/12/06/magazine/white-debt.html

Bebout, L. (2012). The nativist Aztlan: Fantasies and anxieties of whiteness on the border. *Latino Studies, 10*(3), 290–313.

Beech, J. (2004). Redneck and hillbilly discourse in the writing classroom: Classifying critical pedagogies of whiteness. *College English, 67*(2), 32–36.

Behm, N., & Miller, K. D. (2012). Challenging the frameworks of color-blind racism: Why we need a fourth wave of writing assessment. In A. Inoue & M. Poe (Eds.), *Race and writing assessment* (pp. 127–138). Lang.

Bell Jr., D. A. (1992). *Faces at the bottom of the well: The permanence of racism*. Basic.

Bonilla-Silva, E. (2013). *Racism without racists: Color-blind racism and the peristance of racial inequality in America* (4th ed.). Rowman and Littlefield.

Brodkin, K. (1998). *How Jews became White folks & what that says about race in America*. Rutgers University Press.

Brown, C. S. (2002). *Refusing racism: White allies and the struggle for civil rights*. Teachers College Press.

Brown, M. K., et al. (2005). *Whitewashing race: The myth of a color-blind society*. University of California Press.

Bush, M. E. L. (2004). *Breaking the code of good intentions: Everyday forms of whiteness*. Rowman and Littlefield.

Carter, J. B. (2007). *The heart of whiteness: Normal sexuality and race in America, 1880–1940*. Duke University Press.

Castango, A. E. (2008). 'I don't want to hear that!' Legitimating whiteness through silence in schools. *Anthropology and Education Quarterly, 39*(3), 314–333.

Childs, E. C. (2009). *Fade to Black and White: Interracial images in popular culture*. Rowman and Littlefield.

Clark, D. A., & Reed, T. D. (2010). A future we wish to see: Racialized communities studies after White racial anxiety and resentment. *Black Scholar, 40*(4), 37–49.

Coates, T.-N. (2015a). *Between the world and me*. Spiegel and Grau.

Coates, T.-N. (2015b, July/August). There is no post-racial America. *The Atlantic*. Retrieved from https://www.theatlantic.com/magazine/archive/2015/07/post-racial-society-distant-dream/395255/

Coates, T.-N. (2017a, October). The first White president. *The Atlantic*. Atlantic Media Company. Retrieved from http://www.theatlantic.com/magazine/archive/2017/10/the-first-white-presidentta-nehisi-coates/537909/

Coates, T.-N. (2017b). *We were eight years in power: An American tragedy*. One World.

Cooks, L. M., & Simpson, J. S. (Eds.). (2007). *Whiteness, pedagogy, performance: Dis/placing race*. Lexington Books.

Cushman, E. (2012). *The Cherokee Syllabary: Writing the people's perseverance*. University of Oklahoma Press.

Daniels, J. (2009). *Cyber racism: White supremacy online and the new attack on civil rights*. Rowman and Littlefield.

Delgado, R., & Stefanicic, J. (Eds.). (1997). *Critical whiteness studies: Looking beyond the mirror*. Temple University Press.

Delgado, R., & Stefancic, J. (2012). *Critical race theory: An introduction* (2nd ed.). New York University Press.

DiAngelo, R. (2012). *What does it mean to be White? Developing White racial literacy*. Lang.

DiAngelo, R. (2018). *White fragility: Why it's so hard for White people to talk about racism*. Beacon.

Doane, A. W., & Bonilla-Silva, E. (Eds.). (2003). *White out: The continuing significance of racism*. Routledge.

Dryer, R. (1997). *White: Essays on race and culture*. Routledge.

Du Bois, W. E. B. (1998). *Black reconstruction in America, 1860–1880*. Free Press.

Du Bois, W. E. B. (2019). *The souls of Black folk: The unabridged classic*. Clydesdale.

DuVernay, A. (Dir.). (2019). *When they see us*. Netflix.

Emerson, M. O., & Smith, C. (2001). *Divided by faith: Evangelical religion and the problem of race in America*. Oxford University Press.

Everett, A. (Ed.). *Learning race and ethnicity: Youth and digital media*. MIT Press.

Fanon, F. (2008). *Black skins, White masks. 1952*. Grove Press.

Faust, D. G. (2015, December 17). John Hope Franklin: Race and the meaning of America. *New York Review of Books*.

Feagin, J. R., Vera, H., & Batur, P. (2000). *White racism*. Routledge.

Fine, M., et al. (2004). *Echoes of Brown: Youth documenting and performing the legacy of Brown v. Board of Education*. Teachers College Press.

Fine, M., et al. (2004). *Off White: Readings on power, privilege, and resistance* (2nd ed.). Routledge.

Frankenberg, R. (1993). *White women/race matters: The social construction of whiteness*. University of Minnesota Press.

Gaines, J. (1990). White privilege and looking relations: Race and gender in feminist film theory. In P. Erens (Ed.), *Issues in feminist film criticism* (pp. 197–214). Indiana University Press.

Garcia, C. O., Young, V. A., & Pimental, C. (Eds.). (2014). *From "Uncle Tom's cabin" to "the help": Critical perspectives on White-authored narratives of Black life*. Palgrave Macmillan.

Goodburn, A. (1999). Racing (erasing) White privilege in teacher/researcher writing about race. In K. Gilliard (Ed.), *Race, rhetoric, and composition*. Boynton/Cook.

Grzanka, P. R., & Maher, J. (2012). Different, like everyone else: Stuff White people like and the marketplace of diversity. *Symbolic Interaction, 35*(3), 368–393.

Guglielmo, J., & Salerno, S. (Eds.). (2003). *Are Italians White? How race is made in America*. Routledge.

Harris, C. (1993). Whiteness as property. *Harvard Law Review, 106*, 1709–1037.

Hastie, B., & Rimmington, D. (2014). '200 years of White affirmative action': White privilege and discourse in discussions of racial inequality. *Discourse and Society, 25*(2), 186–204.

Hill, D. (2017). *White awake: An honest look at what it means to be White*. IVP Books.

Hill, M. (Ed.). (1997). *Whiteness: A critical reader*. New York University Press.

Holmes, D. G. (2007). Affirmative reaction: Kennedy, Nixon, King, and the evolution of color-blind rhetoric. *Rhetoric Review, 26*(1), 25–41.

hooks, b. (1992). *Black looks: Race and representation*. South End Press.

hooks, b. (2012). *Writing beyond race: Living theory and practice*. Routledge.

Howard, G. R. (1999). *We can't teach what we don't know: White teachers, multi-racial schools*. Teachers College Press.

Hughes, L. (1934). *The ways of White folks*. Alfred A. Knopf.

Ignatiev, N. (1995). *How the Irish became White*. Routledge.

Ignatiev, N., & Garvey, J. (1996). *Race traitor anthology*. Routledge.

Jackson, M. (2006). The enthymematic hegemony of whiteness: The enthymeme as antiracist rhetorical strategy. *JAC, 26*(3–4), 601–641.

Jay, G. (2015). Queer children and representative men: Harper Lee, racial liberalism, and the dilemma of to kill a mockingbird. *American Literary History, 27*(3), 487–522.

Jay, G. (2017). *White writers, race matters: Fictions of racial liberation from Stowe to Stockett*. Oxford University Press.

Keating, A. (1995). Interrogating 'whiteness,' (de)constructing 'race.' *College English, 57*(8) 901–918.

Kendall, F. E. (2006). *Understanding White privilege: Creating pathways to authentic relationships across race*. Routledge.

Kennedy, T. M. (2007). Enthymematical, epistemic, and emotional silence(s) in the rhetoric of whiteness. *JAC, 27,* 253–275.

Kennedy, T. M. (2014, Summer). Sustaining White homonormativity: The kids are all right as public pedagogy. *Journal of Lesbian Studies, 18*(2), 118–132.

Kennedy, T. M., Middleton, J. I., & Ratcliffe, K. (Eds.). (2005). Whiteness studies: Symposium. *Rhetoric Review, 24*(4), 354–402.

King, J. E. (1991). Disconscious racism: Ideology, identity, and the miseducation of teachers. *Journal of Negro Education, 60*(2), 133–146.

Kivel, P. (1996). *Uprooting racism: How White people can work for racial justice*. New Society Publishers.

Lee, V., & Helfand, J. (Eds.). (2005). *Identifying race and transforming whiteness in the classroom*. Peter Lang.

Leonard, D. J. (2015). Remixing the burden: Kony 2012 and the wages of whiteness. *Critical Race and Whiteness Studies, 11*(1), 1–22.

Leonardo, Z. (2004). The color of supremacy: Beyond the discourse of White privilege. *Educational Philosophy and Theory, 36*(2), 137–153.

Lewis, A. E. (2004). 'What group'? Studying whites and whiteness in the era of 'color-blindness.' *Sociological Theory, 22*(4), 623–646.

Lipsitz, G. (1998). *The possessive investment in whiteness: How White people profit from identity politics*. Temple University Press.

Lopez, I. H. (1996). *White by law: The legal construction of race*. New York University Press.

Lopez, I. H. (2014). *Dog whistle politics: How coded racial appeals have reinvented racism and wrecked the middle class*. Oxford University Press.

Martinez, A. Y. (2009). 'The American way': Resisting the empire of force and color-blind racism. *College English, 71*(6), 584–595.

McCarthy, C. (2003). Contradictions of power and identity: Whiteness studies and the call of teacher education. *Qualitative Studies in Education, 19*(1), 127–133.

McCarthy, C., & Crichlow, W. (Eds.). (1993). *Race, identity, and representation in education*. Routledge.

McDermott, M. (2006). *Working-class White: The making and unmaking of race relations*. University of California Press.

McIntyre, A. (2000). Antiracist pedagogy in the university: The ethical challenges of making whiteness public. In M. Brabeck (Ed.), *Practicing feminist ethics in psychology* (pp. 55–74). APA.

McIntyre, A. (2008). Engaging diverse groups of colleagues in conversation. In M. Pollock (Ed.), *Everyday antiracism: Getting real about race in school* (pp. 279–282). Harvard University Press.

McIntyre, A. (1997). *Making meaning of whiteness: Exploring racial identity with White teachers.* State University of New York.

McIntosh, P. (1988). *White privilege and male privilege: A personal account of coming to see correspondences through work in women's studies.* Wellesley College Center for Research on Women.

McIntosh, P. (2007). White privilege: Unpacking the invisible knapsack. In P. S. Rothberg (Ed.), *Race, class, and gender in the United States: An integrated study* (7th ed., pp. 177–182). Worth Publishers.

McMorris, M. (2015). I was an honorary White man: Reflections on space, place, and origin. In B. Bergo & T. Nicholls (Eds.), *I don't see color: Personal and critical perspectiveson White privilege.* The Pennsylvania State University Press.

Metzel, J. M. (2019). *Dying of whiteness: How the politics of racial resentment is killing America's heartland.* Basic Books.

Mills, C. W. (1999). *The racial contract.* Cornell University Press.

Morrison, T. (1992). *Playing in the dark: Whiteness and the literary imagination.* Vintage Books.

Morton-Robinson, A., Casey, M., & Nicholl, F. (Eds.). (2008). *Transnational whiteness matters: Mythunderstanding.* Rowman and Littlefield.

Nakamura, L. (2002). *Cybertypes: Race, ethnicity, and identity on the internet.* Routledge.

Nakamura, L., & Chow-White, P. A. (Eds.). (2012). *Race after the internet.* Routledge.

Nakayama, T., & Krizek, R. (1995). Whiteness: A strategic rhetoric. *Quarterly Journal of Speech, 81*(3), 291–309.

Ogbu, J. (1991). Cultural diversity and school experience. In C. E. Walsh (Ed.), *Literacy as praxis: Culture, language, and pedagogy* (pp. 25–50). Ablex.

Okrent, D. (2019). *The guarded gate: Bigotry, eugenics, and the law that kept two generations of Jew, Italians, and Other European immigrants out of America.* Scribner.

O'Neill, O. (1996). Introduction. In C. M. Korsgaard (Ed.), *The sources of normativity.* Cambridge University Press.

Painter, N. I. (2010). *The history of White people.* Norton.

Parker, M. (2017). *There are more beautiful things than beyonce.* Tin House Books.

Prendergast, C. (2003). *Literacy and racial justice: The politics of learning after Brown v. Board of Education.* Southern Illinois University Press.

Prendergast, C. (1998). Race: The absent presence in composition studies. *College Composition and Communication, 50*(1), 36–53.

Powell, A. H. (2017). Reflection: 'Postracial.' In T. M. Kennedy, J. I. Middleton, & K. Ratcliffe (Eds.), *Rhetorics of whiteness* (pp. 19–21). Southern Illinois University Press.

Rankine, C. (2014). *Citizen: An American lyric*. Graywolf Press.

Ratcliffe, K. (1999). Eavesdropping as rhetorical tactic: History, whiteness, and rhetoric. *JAC: A Journal of Composition Theory, 20*(1), 195–244.

Ratcliffe, K. (Eds.). (2005). *Rhetorical listening: Identification, gender, whiteness*. Southern Illinois University Press.

Ratcliffe, K. (2007). In search of the unstated: The enythymeme and/of whiteness. *JAC, 27*, 275–290.

Roediger, D. R. (1991). *The wages of whiteness: Race and the making of the American working class*. Verso.

Roediger, D. R. (Ed.). (1998). *Black on White: Black writers on what it means to be White*. Schocken.

Roediger, D. R. (2005). *Working towards whiteness: How America's immigrants became White; The strange journey from Ellis Island to the suburbs*. Basic Books.

Ross, T. R. (1990). The rhetorical tapestry of race. *William and Mary Law Review, 32*.

Rothenberg, P. S. (Ed.). (2002). *White privilege: Essential readings on the other side of racism*. Worth.

Rothenberg, P. S. (2007). *Race, class, and gender in the United States* (7th ed.). Worth.

Rothstein, R. (2017). *The color of law: A forgotten history of how our government segretated housing*. Liveright.

Ryden, W., & Marshall, I. (2012). *Reading, writing, and the rhetorics of whiteness*. Routledge.

Sechrest, L. L. (2018). *Can "White" people be saved? Triangulating Race, theology, and mission*. IVP Academic.

Segrest, M. (1999). *Memoir of a race traitor*. South End Press.

Shotwell, A. (2011). *Knowing otherwise: Race, gender, and implicit understanding*. Pennsylvania State University Press.

Simien, J. (Dir.), Williams, T. J., Thompson, T., & Gallner, K. (Performers). (2014). *Dear White people*. Code Red.

Sleeter, C. E. (2001). Preparing teachers for culturally diverse schools: Research and the overwhelming presence of whiteness. *Journal of Teacher Education, 52*(2), 94–106.

Sleeter, C. E. (2011). Becoming White: Reinterpreting a family story by putting race back into the picture. *Race Ethnicity and Education, 14*(4), 421–433.

Smedley, A., & Smedley, B. D. (2012). *Race in North America: Origin and evolution of a worldview* (4th ed.). Westview Press.

Smith, P. (2004, Spring). Whiteness, normal theory, and disability studies. *Disability Studies Quarterly, 24*(2).

Steele, C. (2011). *Whistling Vivaldi: How stereotypes affect us and what we can do.* W. W. Norton and Company.

Taylor, G. (2005). *Buying whiteness: Race, culture, and identity from Columbus to hip-hop.* Palgrave Macmillan.

Thandeka. (2000). *Learning to be White: Money, race and god in America.* Continuum.

Thompson, C., Schaeffer, E., & Brod, H. (Eds.). (2003). *White men challenging racism: 35 personal stories.* Duke University Press.

Trainor, J. S. (2002). Critical pedagogy's 'other': Constructions of whiteness in education for social change. *College Composition and Communication, 53*(4), 631–650.

Trainor, J. S. (2008). *Rethinking racism: Emotion, persuasion, and literacy education in an all-White suburban high school.* Southern Illinois University Press.

Ward, J. (2008). White normativity: The cultural dimensions of whiteness in a racially diverse LGBT organization. *Sociological Perspectives, 51*(3), 563–586.

Ward, J. (2015). *Not GAY: Sex between straight White men.* New York University Press.

Warner, M. (1999). *The trouble with normal: Sex, politics, and the ethics of queer life.* The Free Press.

Watson, V. T. (2013). *The souls of White folk: African-American writers theorize whiteness.* University Press of Mississippi.

West, C. (1994). *Race matters.* Vintage.

Williams, P. J. (1991). *The alchemy of race and rights.* Harvard University Press.

Wills, J. (1996). Who needs multicultural education? White students, U.S. history, and the construction of a usable past. *Anthropology and Education Quarterly, 27*(3), 365–389.

Winans, A. (2010). Cultivating racial literacy in White, segregated settings: Emotions as site of ethical engagement and inquiry. *Curriculum Inquiry, 40*(3), 475–491.

Wing, A. K. (Ed.). (2003). *Critical race feminism: A reader.* New York University Press.

Wise, T. (2010). *Color-blind: The rise of post-racial politics and the retreat from racial equality.* City Lights Books.

Wise, T. (2011). *White like me: Reflection on race from a privileged son.* Soft Skull Press.

Wise, T. (2012). *Dear White America: Letter to a new minority.* City Lights Publishers.

Wray, M., & Newitz, A. (Eds.). (1997). *White trash: Race and class in America.* Routledge.

Yancy, G. (Ed.). (2004). *What White looks like: African-American philosophers on the White question.* Routledge.

www.ingramcontent.com/pod-product-compliance
Lightning Source LLC
Chambersburg PA
CBHW061419300426
44114CB00015B/1996